It's Never Too Late

CW00821022

Anthony Fox

chipmunkapublishing
the mental health publisher

Published by
Chipmunkapublishing
United Kingdom

http://www.chipmunkapublishing.com

ISBN 978-1-78382-009-2

Chipmunkapublishing gratefully acknowledge the support of Arts Council England.

Remember

"To ourselves all the lies we told.
All the dreams we sold.
Once we were young, now it's real fun.
The story foretold we were not cold.
The past is gone, the future long.
Remember this!"

Poem written by Anthony Fox © 1999

It's Never Too Late

I want to say thank you to all the people who have encouraged me to write this book, especially my bank manager, no I'm only joking. But, seriously most people don't read this bit, but I think a thank you is important to acknowledge the help and support family and friends have given. I like to say special thanks for the encouragement that my daughter Colleen and my son Jamie have given me over the time it has taken me to write this book.

This book is not a medical remedy for bipolar, but a collection of stories that reflect my experience and viewpoint that I hope will sometimes make you laugh and possibly help you reflect on your life. I swing on a tree between two extremes; black and white or Jekyll and Hyde. But life's a bitch, right! But living with bi-polar disorder is even more of a roller coaster ride. As you will see…

Contents

Introduction   7

Does Fate Control Our Lives?   11

Breaking the Cycle   19

The Journey's Long, and Only with Yourself   27

Do You Believe in Miracles or Luck?   41

Love is Everything   47

Confidence Lets Talk   53

Chasing the Circle Equals Never Being Satisfied   59

Opportunity Knocked at My Door   65

I Didn't Believe in Taking Shortcuts   69

Bipolar Thinking – Critical Thinking   75

A Mirage – Things You Can't See   83

Changing My Perspective   89

The Truth Never Lies   93

A Different Kind of Love   97

The Black Cloud that Surrounds Me   101

Predict the Future   107

The Butterfly and the Bee   111

Living with Bipolar   115

Live the Dream   119

Just a Few Pennies More	125
I Took the Plunge	131
Getting Old Sucks!	135
End of the Book	139

Introduction

"Help others achieve their dreams and you will achieve yours,"
by Les Brown

Please, before you read this book don't judge if you don't know me. Maybe when you have read this book you may want to criticise what I have written. Even then I don't think you will fully understand, because I don't even understand myself sometimes. Because I live with bipolar disorder a chronic condition that apparently affects over 1% of the population. It's a condition that has plagued me with a black cloud of depression most of my life, I believe.

My story will take you from the streets of America as a young boy to a discovery in the jungle of India to an enlightenment and maturity of the present day in England.

It's a truthful account about my experience combined with a street philosophy as a way of looking at life with open eyes. Some of the stories I shall tell may shock or question your belief but try to keep an open mind. We all have that survival instinct so let your mind free and become a survivor.

As we travel through my life looking at fate, luck, love, money and many more interesting subjects you will find the philosophy that should be helpful in your life. Out of every negative comes some positives; its natures balance. Be careful what you wish for though, because as you will see dreams do come true.

I will show you how poor decisions can have lasting affects and how mistakes we make sometimes show us the path we must lead. I wish I didn't make so many mistakes but then the saying goes "*it is said that only a fool learns from his own mistakes, a wise man from the mistakes of others*, "an anonymous quote.

Now, don't go jumping of a bridge, though, that's not a bad idea, only joking.

To me it seems that we all strive constantly for more each day, whether that's more material wealth or just a better understanding of who we are and why we are here. Yet, when we depart this world we leave with nothing of earthly value.

The only real worth is the love we have encountered in our life. This book is about love and finding who we really are. The kind of philosophy and experience I have learnt will possibly help you in your life, I sincerely hope so.

How I came to write this book is some ways is the result of being hospitalised. No. Not because I was writing a book that happened later. I mean the computer didn't blow up and put me in hospital, although at times I have felt like chucking my laptop straight out the window. I have less patience now with computers than a dog on heat.

You can call me Tony, so let the story begin...

Does Fate Control Our Lives?

"Coincidence is God's way of remaining anonymous,"
by Albert Einstein

Fate is described as a predetermined event or series of events outside our control as is synonymous with your destiny, and or part of the order of the cosmos. We can describe what fate is but do we really understand what it means? Do you believe in a spiritual fate that predetermines your destiny? I ask this question because we all live on that knife edge of reality.

The science establishment is still debating whether our universe is deterministic or not. Ever since the big bang event everything that has happened in our universe has been determined by this event. Some philosophers have a different view within which they argue that there's an unseen force we call fate.

For example, think about gravity it's an unseen force which affects our lives in all sorts of ways, such as the movement of tides or how heavy we are. There's a lot we don't understand and fate ends up being the fall guy sometimes.

It was 1970, and it feels fresh today in my memory when I left America for England alone as a 12 year old boy all those years ago to live with my grandparents in England after my mum and dad had separated.

I remember the tearful goodbye at *John F. Kennedy* airport, how my younger brother cried with my mother desperately upset, and me feeling empty not wanting to leave. My mother wasn't coping with my younger brother and me, since my dad had disappeared with his secretary to the state of Texas, the oil rich middle of America.

The only salvation was my grandmother in England. My grandparents in England had offered to help but couldn't take both my brother and me. Fate had intervened, and it had a way of slapping you in the face.

Why does fate take hold when least expected or was it there all the time waiting to guide me along a path? I wasn't sure.

So it was just me taking that lonely walk onto the airplane that day with the promise that it wouldn't be that long before we would be all re-united again. I didn't want to leave America I had friends and a life.

Playing American football in the park after school and hanging around the local pizza parlour were everyday activities for me. For a few quarters you could buy a slice of real Italian pizza, and slosh it down with a rootbeer.

We would watch the traffic go back and forth along Main Street and discuss the girls in our class and not much else before we had to get back home, and do our boring homework. On the walk to school I would stop by the deli for a hot bagel and a freshly made chocolate milkshake.

America had a different smell to England that's for sure. Hot humid summers and dry snowy winters made it so that we always had something to do every season. There was pumpkin pie in the autumn and always water melon to cool us down in the summer while our parents celebrated Independence Day in the park. I was happy with the American way of life but upset that my parents had now gone their separate ways.

Arriving at Heathrow airport I wasn't happy to see my grandmother. On the drive from the airport to north London where my grandparents lived all I could think about was what I had left behind.

Everything in England looked smaller from the cars to the roads to all the shops crammed together. I hadn't remembered much about England except the rain. On my face was an angry disposition my grandmother couldn't understand.

Although, I was born in England I didn't feel English the last six years or so living in America made sure of that, and before that living in Wollongong, a city just south of Sydney, Australia.

I don't remember much about living in Australia I was too young, other than the kangaroos and boomerangs and the day a spider crawled out of the sand and bit me on the arm. For some reason I didn't tell my parents for several days until they noticed I was constantly holding my arm across my chest. Luckily for me it wasn't a deadly poisonous bite otherwise I would not be telling my story.

Living in England was a big change for me, everything seemed so small I was used to the enormous mega department stores of New Jersey on route 46, where you could walk all day around the aisles and buy anything you dreamed if you had the money. America was the home of the 4x4, and butter salted popcorn, and the outside drive-in movie theatres of New Jersey where mum and dad would take us sometimes to see a film.

All I could think of was what I was missing, my friends, girls, pizza and the deli and everything American, even the smell. The closest thing you could call a big store in England at that time was Woolworth's the place where you could spend your pocket money on Meccano, and that was just about it. There was some compensation being in England, I would hang around the local cafe on the north circular. My favourite meal was egg and chips; I used to like dipping my chips into a soft egg, they made the tastiest chips. And, after that, have a go on the pin ball wizard machine I was always ready to take a spin. I was always trying to beat a previous high score, which was the addiction of the pinball wizard game.

Schools were different too. I went from top of class to the bottom in the space of a year. I just wasn't interested. My grandmother had placed me in a school just for boys. This was something I wasn't used to, all my previous schools I had a chance to mix with girls. Instead of a leisurely walk to school it had become a transport marathon to get to school. I would get on a bus to catch the train and then run to catch the underground tube and finally another bus before I was finally at school. I became withdrawn and felt more isolated lost in an empty shell.

About a year later my grandfather died which was a shame because I enjoyed the times we spent flying his model airplanes on Hampstead Heath, and the stories he would tell about the war and what inventions he had made. I would always laugh when I saw him driving around in his bubble car which only had one seat, sometimes he would squeeze me in and take me for a ride to the shops.

Riding in a bubble car was like being a mouse and all the other cars were elephants ready to squash us.

It was weird the day my grandfather died. I was at school and all day I had a bad feeling that something terrible had happened I just didn't know what until I got back from school.

The feeling would not go away until my grandmother told me what had happened. My grandfather had hung himself from the ceiling light in the bathroom. I remember a dream I had that night and looking out my window of my bedroom all I could see outside was Skeletons walking in the street below.

I think we all plan our lives and when things go wrong we call into question whether fate had anything to do with it. My grandfather had committed suicide and made his choice. Suicide is interrupting fate it's a choice we make.

Why do we think fate plays its part as if we don't have a choice or the choices we make are only half-choices?

After the funeral my dad returned from America with his fiancée, well that was the term he used at the time. My dad never got to go to the funeral and nor did I.

To this day I do not understand the reasons why my grandmother would not let me go to the funeral, and let me say one last goodbye.

Anyway, my grandmother was glad to see my dad, she had this ridiculous idea that somehow he would stay in England. I didn't think so, but that was me, a doubting Thomas maybe? Over a year and a half had passed since I had last seen my dad since he had left mum and brother and me in New Jersey. I wasn't best pleased to see him, which is how I felt, and I told him so.

After dad had finished ransacking my grandmother's home of all grandpas' possessions such as his airplanes, books and even his watch there wasn't much left to remember him by except a few old photographs of him flying his model airplanes?

Anyway, dad had booked a cottage for the week in a place called Hartland, along the North Devon coastline which had a notorious history in the past of ship wreckers and smugglers.

The West Country, as it's affectionately called was a place of small rural farms and hedgerows amongst winding roads about 6 hours drive south west from London, if you know the roads.

So there we were granny and I, dad and his fiancée all packed into a Hillman Hunter a relatively small car, and ready for the gruelling drive from London to the West Country, a place I had never seen before.

Never experiencing much of England's rich and green countryside of small fields separated by cobbled walls and bramble hedgerows it was a child's adventure playground. Totally different from what I had been use to.

I had grown up in the urban jungle of the heart land of cities far away from the peaceful idyllic countryside. Hartland was indeed a place of history and mystery where some of the cottages had demons cast in plaster which adorned the tops of their doorways, the local church had old trees so bent they took the shape of the devil's horns.

On the beautiful yet rugged coast line you could imagine where the ship wreckers would steer unsuspecting ships to the depths of the merciless sea. Any survivors would have been killed for their bounty. It was a tightknit community then and even today you could hear locals thinking: *You're not from around here, and I can tell.*

It was just another day, everyone was crammed into the car to go site seeing along the coast of North Devon and Cornwall. It wasn't long before we stopped at a roadside cafe not far from Hartland into the county of Cornwall at a place called Bude.

Strangely, it was then that I had this feeling deep within the pit of my stomach that I had been there before. The cafe was nothing special to look at with rickety old signs flapping in the wind that had seen better days. Deserted and shabby the cafe had an eerie feel like you see in those films of outback roadside stops where people go in and never come out again. That is how it felt, creepy. But, like I said before, I had never been to the West Country in my life.

The whole experience is as fresh today as if it only happened yesterday. As we all got out the car, the location seemed familiar. *I'd been here before*, I kept thinking. It felt so bizarre, the whole experience, I knew what was going to happen. Every step we took I knew before it happened. Had fate brought me to this place for a reason?

As we entered the cafe the entire place looked familiar inside, and it was a weird experience as we all sat round a table, waiting to be served. The cafe was empty except for us but as I looked at the decor, the way the tables were arranged, the advertising signs, in fact, everything felt as if I knew it like the back of my hand. I even said to my dad, '*it feels like I've been here before,*' but I hadn't. My dad's reply was, "*it's probably Déjà vu,*" I asked him what it meant. My dad explained, but at the same time had a way of putting me down for not knowing what it meant.

I told everyone what would happen next, that a young waitress would come out with dark hair and her name would be Susan. And, indeed, a young dark haired waitress maybe a little bit older than me did come to our table, and her name was Susan. Everyone was spooked except for me as everything felt so familiar. I felt I knew the young waitress so much that when we had to leave I could not help thinking that I would meet that girl again someday. Yet, it felt we had already met before today somehow.

Even today my spiritual intuition if I can call it that has always been strong. Ever since childhood my ability to see and feel strange things has been part of my life.

I know that *Déjà vu* is a phenomenon that is not fully understood by science but this is no surprise as there are many esoteric intangibles that science cannot explain. I believe that fate and *Déjà vu* maybe closely related in as much as they both relate to events, one to a future event(s) and the other to an event(s) in the past and yet you experience that event in the present or at least that is how it feels.

Is everything predetermined? Yet, my grandfather had committed suicide a choice he made, which ultimately brought my father back to England and made him choose to travel to the West Country. I had experienced *Déjà vu* in a part of the world I had never been to before. Was this fate or did we have choices all along? I'm not sure; I will let you think about that for a while.

I believe that we have choices, but I am not so sure if we can determine our own destiny. Remember the chaos theory of the universe which has been proved to show deterministic patterns even though they are hard to see at first but they are there. Maybe this is what we encounter as fate? I will let you decide...

Breaking the Cycle

"The best proof of love is trust,"
by Joyce Brothers

I was not quite 14 years old, and plagued with the usual teenage facial spots where more seemed to sprout each morning that I looked in the mirror. I was conscious of my appearance, not particularly vain, but you never knew when a girl would catch your eye.

I was always conscious of those few freckles that would appear on my face in the summer time, and then would fade as winter came along. I remember it all began with a bully at school in America, who would always call me names, and one of the names stuck in my head, '*freckle face*,' he would say. Strange, isn't it how some insignificant words can have a lasting affect? It wasn't only my freckles that would taunt me. My dark brown curly hair, which everyone would love except for me, was difficult to comb, and would often look more like a straggly floor mop than a head of hair.

The early confidence I had in America had vanished. I wasn't the budding confident boy entrepreneur anymore who was always finding ways to make pocket money in school, by selling fancy rubber pen and pencil tops that I would make at home in the kitchen with the toy oven I had received one Christmas. I was always busy in the winters when the snows came where I would clear people's drives and show my brother what to do, and in the hot summers I would set up a stall on the pavement outside our house and sell lemonade to passer-by's.

It was always a venture so I could buy some pizza or the White Castle burgers which was just on the corner down of our street. But, all the initial promise had gone since the move to London. I had withdrawn and wasn't confident anymore. I didn't have my parents around to praise me, and I never trusted my grandmother's words or the false love she had for me. She could praise you in one sentence, and in the next belittle it with another hurtful comment, it was her usual way.

My dad was the same as his mother he had a way of knocking you back, and making you look small, especially in front of other people. In later years, he would say to my son Jamie, *'you have a chip on your shoulder'* which was a comment I didn't like. I knew some insignificant words could have a lasting affect on a child. It was the same kind of shit and put downs he had said to me.

Later, I would learn to keep my son and daughter away from dad and my grandmother as much as possible. When you are young and venerable you start to believe what you are told, it can take a long time to undo the damage and break the cycle. I know this because it took many years for me to rid myself of the hurt, and the things that had been said to me by my grandmother and my dad.

In some ways I wasn't sad when my dad left us in America, I was sort of glad. I remember the fights and arguments my dad would have with mum, and my brother and me barricading ourselves in a room for protection. Our dad would be kind one minute and mean and nasty the next and that's the only way to describe him.

Looking back, I remember when we were all sat round the table for dinner one summer's day. My brother made a comment about something he didn't want to eat, and suddenly without warning my dad slapped him across the face so hard you could see blood seeping from his ear.

As I reflect back to those years, I can see it was the adults around me who failed to adequately look after me. But my in-built safety mechanism would kick in and I would bury the trauma for now, which would help me break the cycle of a dad who didn't care and of a grandmother who said she loved me, but did everything to hate her.

They say that there are two schools of thought; that bipolar is a product of your environment, and or a defective gene, a chemical imbalance. As my dad and my grandfather suffered with manic depression, and it's also more than likely I have inherited the condition, which as you read my story you will see what hell this has caused me. But even with this disorder throughout my life I would battle with my demons not to be like my grandmother and my dad, because I did care. I knew love came from the heart and even from an early age I had it. And I had to break the cycle.

Anyway, before granny sold the house in London to be camped closer to where dad was now living in the West Country we were off to Gower peninsular a part of Wales for a summer holiday.

Granny was Welsh so it was no surprise she wanted to visit the places she had been to as a child.

It began on one of those holidays that seem to linger in your memory forever. I can see it now, as if it was only yesterday, still fresh as the summer breeze that gently cooled our sun baked bodies as we lay on the beach of golden sands. Chastity of love, no broken trusts just a memory as pure as falling snow. Fresh as daises cut, those sweet lips that kissed. Oh! I still linger to taste those lips on that first kiss.

Sometimes you meet someone in your life for a very short time, but that memory lasts and you think to yourself will we ever meet again? Even at the time it felt odd, I wanted to know if we would ever meet again there was something telling me in my mind and heart not to let go. Maybe I didn't understand my feelings.

Maybe it was the first time I felt love, I know my stomach had more butterflies than bees in a hive. Now, I know it was a feeling of love in which I could trust, which was something I couldn't do with my grandmother and my dad.

The first time we met we both seemed to know each other because that is how it felt. There was no nagging doubt, just comfortable. I still feel even now how special it was the time we had together.

I remember not feeling awkward about my appearance, as if however I looked she liked and I was pleased. I guess in many ways it was the first time for a long time that I felt anyone loved me for who I was. She was American girl from California, and I still had my American accent combined with some north London brogue picked up already.

Karen had that sandy brown hair and blue eyes with that west coast accent and a tan that I so loved. Both of us were staying at the same hotel and holidaying at the Gower Peninsular near Three Cliffs Bay, which had a fantastic beach of golden sands where we would spend our days playing, and hiding from her parents and my grandmother.

I couldn't wait to see her in the mornings at breakfast time. Karen would see me and a smile would exchange between us. Occasionally, we would kiss each other in the little secret time we had together on the beach or at the hotel out of sight of her parents and my grandmother. When our hands would touch and the sensation of love would cascade throughout my body from head to toe. The fun of her smile and the laughter in her voice is what captured my heart. There was no thought of breaking that trust we had, we were in love that is all that mattered.

Yes, we were young, but we both knew without having to that the trust was there. I didn't want to let go, inside I felt like our holiday together should go on and on. Maybe it was the first time I had experienced love, but whatever it was I wanted more? I would miss that smile on her face and that warmth I felt inside.

It was a love I could trust. A love not sallied by chains of duty, not reckless in its pursuit, an open love not parked with doubt, just an honesty of youth.

I wanted to go back to America and somehow be with Karen. I knew I couldn't but that is what I wanted. There was no trust to break in our love, we were only young, not yet old enough to make promises we could not keep. But still that love shone like a bright candle between us, for there was something of magic glue that kept us together, sweetness of honey, a purity of love.

On the last day we had together, we said our goodbyes, and I can remember Karen's words she said to me, *'goodbye Tony, I hope we meet again.'* A sweet kiss touched our lips, and loves shadow was gone. I had bid farewell to a love I could trust, and hoped it would come ashore again.

A few more months had passed before we were living in the bungalow granny had bought in Appledore, North Devon not far from the village where my dad and his fiancée had lived for a few months before vanishing.

My dad, well he had disappeared back to the States we surmised. Granny and I had taken a ride out one day to see them only to find they had sold the brand new house granny had bought them and vanished without as much as a phone call or a letter. I had a feeling my dad had gone but granny would not believe me. My dad had sold everything and didn't leave a trace of where and when he had gone.

Granny and dad never got on with each other, its fair to say my dad just hated his mother, and now I can see why in many ways. I remember one day before the bungalow was finished granny and I turning up at the doorstep of the house she had bought for her son only to find dad had no intention of letting her in. A furious argument ensued. We had driven several hours from the south coast of Devon to view the progress of the bungalow being built in Appledore.

At the time we were staying in a hotel in Torquay until the bungalow was finished. Granny was expecting her son to put us up for the night. Well, he did but only on the floor without a pillow or a blanket. My dad just didn't care. At the time I just did not understand why they could not get on and why he hated her so much.

Appledore was a small fishing village on the mouth of the Tamar estuary and on the hill where we lived you could see the Atlantic Ocean. I always longed to be back in America where for most of the time I had been happy. There wasn't much in Appledore just an old church and a few small shops. It had become more of a tourist location, a place to visit and wander round the narrow cobbled streets and view the quaint white washed cottages.

The word Appledore was derived from the Saxon word Apuldre (meaning an apple tree) as the locals would tell you.

Each week granny and I would travel the few miles to Bideford an old port town on the Taw River, to buy groceries in the only supermarket at that time. Working on the checkout I would see this girl. I always wanted to talk to her and ask her for a date but always lost my nerve. Back then I was the shy type always not sure of myself and to be honest I don't think I have changed that much. Maybe, just a tad more confident especially with girls.

She was the kind of girl I had never met in Appledore, even though I had joined a local youth club everyone stuck to each other like in a clan, Appledorian's did not like outsiders. I still had an American accent that did not help. From her accent I could tell she was not local, and there was always that feeling I wanted to date her because of that. I always felt we would make a good couple, a pair of outsiders in a tightknit community.

She reminded me of American girls for some reason, maybe it was the way she set her sandy brown hair or the use of make-up that matched her light green eyes. She appeared more American to me and that is all that mattered when she gave me a smile and said hello. American girls would give me the impression of being more like their mothers, maybe they were more mature, either way she would break my heart.

Every week I would make sure I would steer granny's shopping cart down her aisle, so I had a chance to say hello and smile. I would exchange a few words but would always lose my nerve to ask her out. Looking back maybe I feared rejection, and I am not sure. It was probably the fear of what my grandmother would say, she would have said something to put me down on the spot.

But each week I found out more. Her name was Tanya and she came from the midlands a largely industrial part of England. In some ways I was slow, but I was getting to know her and enjoying my weekly visits.

Anyway, after many weeks of just smiles and saying hello, I plucked up enough courage to ask her out. I was gutted the day she told me that she was moving away with her parents that week to another part of the country. And, I never saw her again. But, I learnt a valuable lesson from that experience. If I had not lost my confidence since the move to England, I am sure I would have asked her out earlier.

But, fear of what maybe my grandmother would say, because she would often say things in front of other people to put me down I didn't take the risk, until it's was too late. I didn't know it then, but I was learning to break the cycle of not growing up with the shit that my dad and grandmother were always dishing out to me.

It's Never Too Late

The Journey's Long, and Only with Yourself

> *"Literature is mostly about having sex and not much about having children. Life is the other way round."*
> by David Lodge

I was 16 going on 17 years old when I had my stomach pumped in hospital after trying to kill myself with an overdose of sleeping pills. Even then, after all that, the medical profession failed to recognise I suffered from manic depression, and that is when I think I should have been diagnosed with bipolar all those years ago. Sure, I had seen a psychiatrist, and a social worker would come to visit me, but looking back, now, I do not think they believed me. I was well fed and didn't have any outward signs of physical abuse but inside I had been suffering from mental abuse.

They failed to understand what my life was like living with my grandmother who was always constantly angry with me. Adults never want to listen to what children have to say, especially back then, maybe attitudes have changed since then, and I am still not sure.

Although, it's many years ago now, I still remember those early years living with my grandmother, how, I believe she destroyed in me what little confidence I had. How, she would say that I couldn't match up to her beloved Joe, my grandfather. Whatever I did she would always say that her Joe had done better. I wasn't trying to beat anyone just looking for some praise, which I never got.

The suicide attempt had been a reaction to living with my grandmother who was always angry with me. She told me I was the reason my grandfather had killed himself. I didn't find out until many years later that it wasn't me, it was her. My grandfather hadn't been happy with my grandmother for many years. Apparently, he was no angel, with several affairs under his belt. My grandmother would always blame me; she would not take the blame herself.

So there it is I had gone from happy environment to a mentally abusive environment, so then it's no wonder I was ready to end my life. I could not go back to mum in America, she had gotten re-married to a jealous husband who could not stand another man's offspring around the house.

Even my brother ended up living with another family friend. My mum was weak I understand that now, but I also understand her reasons. My mum over the years had told me she had made a big mistake sending me to England, and letting my brother live with another family. When we make mistakes we do not realise the ripples it can have.

The years would pass but the abuse did not stop, not only was granny a wicked old witch sometimes but I also suffered at work. I guess it must be an invisible tattoo across my forehead that only abusers can see. I was weak because the closest people in my life had let me down. Otherwise, it would have been a different story, because I later grew strong knowing I had to. I was serving an apprenticeship as a carpenter with a local building company, a job incidentally that granny had gotten for me, which I never would have dreamed of entering in a million years, and it just wasn't me. But, my grandmother was adamant, she just wouldn't see it any other way than hers.

For two years I worked everyday with this bully of a master carpenter, who was constantly shouting and just plain abusive, I was even more depressed with my life. I complained to granny several times about what was happening to me and even saw the head of the building company neither of them did a thing about the abuse I was suffering. There was no one else I could turn to. My life was hell at times.

Years later I would bump into the abuser who thought I would be all smiles when I saw him, but I was not. I told the old man what I thought of him and told him he should be ashamed at the life he had given me. There had been no handshake I just walked away proud that I hadn't forgotten, and wasn't willing to either...

I was only just 19 years old when I got married to Karen the girl I had met at a local disco a couple of years earlier in Bideford. Karen was quiet and a softly spoken true blond and she always knew what was right and didn't have a bad word to say about anyone. Even today I don't think she has changed much still a caring soul and someone you could always rely on. The first time I met Karen I knew then that she was the girl for me. When I asked her for a dance and her gentle voice said yes there was an immediate intimacy between us. When we were ready to say goodbye that night and I asked if I could walk her home it was a triumph when she said yes, somehow I knew I had found someone special.

On the walk back to her home we talked about this and that, but it was that kiss has we said goodbye that sealed the love that was to blossom over the coming years.

My depression would come and go almost like the seasons. Looking back, now, I can see why. My grandmother was still there in the background, who would try everything she could to spoil the happiness I had found. She didn't like Karen for no other reason than she wanted to rule me like a pawn in a game, and decide what and who was best for me. She had tried to do the same thing with my dad and mum and she had refused to accept my dad's choice and never liked my mum from day one.

History was repeating itself and she would do all she could to spread the same evil she had within her. I have no regrets about getting married at a young age. Yes, my future wife was pestered by her parents to get married, for reasons I still don't know. I didn't have my parents around to take advice. Besides, even if they were around I have trouble listening to myself let alone taking notice of what my parents had to say. My dad's words would always be that he didn't really care and my mum's would have been - do what's right for you. My grandmother's words, well, I never trusted. Besides, I was glad to get away from my grandmother who always wanted to rule my life with words or anger. She could show what looked like love to other people, but underneath that veneer was an evil side. Like the time on my 16th birthday when she bought me a tape recorder player but only to take back of me a few days later when she was angry and wanted her way.

It would be more than 30 years later when I found the tape player tucked away in her bedroom wardrobe as I cleaned out my grandmother's home after she had gone into a care home. Whatever was inside her it wasn't love, I don't really think she understood what it meant.

The wedding was in the local Church of England and I think it went well, even though we were both young. Looking back now, I can see that many things were a reaction to my life with my grandmother. I would often have to barricade myself in my bedroom from granny who would throw a fist into the door. I remember ducking from the odd dinner plate that would fly through the air in my direction. Although, I didn't want my grandmother to turn up at the wedding reception she was there casting her spell.

Karen was a true blond at least until later when she started to darken to a softer brown. She had always had a good complexion to match her angelic face, even today she never looks her age. When I look at our wedding photos now, I can see our love and how happy we were.

What happened in our marriage over the forthcoming years was my fault; I hadn't got over the manic depression that constantly plagued me. The manic depression that would strike at any time was also a constant battle in our marriage. I didn't realise what the problem was until many years later when I started to talk about what had happened to me.

It wasn't long before Karen was pregnant with a baby boy. We named our first James and his second name after my brother Benjamin. We found it difficult knowing what to do at first but we soon realised most of the crying was due to wind. We started calling our son Jamie who had golden blond curls and brown eyes like me.

Karen and I at the time were fond of watching a Scottish TV series which the lead character a James MacAlpine was always referred to as Jamie which was a nickname we both liked. We had been blessed with a healthy and beautiful son. Karen and I were very happy, we didn't realise as young parents how much joy Jamie would bring into our hearts. Even though my depression would always be there in the background the early years of our marriage were happy ones.

Looking back, at times, the early years of our marriage were characterised with a kind of fatalism. In the 80s all you heard on TV and all that what was popping through the letter box was the threat of nuclear war and how to be prepared. You would see how some people had built bomb shelters in their gardens and want to do if you couldn't afford a shelter.

The whole period you felt as if, what's the point, if your world could end at any moment? With the constant talk of nuclear annihilation any hopes and dreams seemed to fade, and my depression would sink me even further into the abyss. Karen and I would talk about if we survived a nuclear attack would it be a world we want to live in.

In the midst of all this madness along came Colleen our beautiful baby girl. We chose to name our daughter with an Irish name because it was unusual and we both liked it, with the second name Rebecca after a favourite second cousin of mine. Colleen soon had a head of hair like Shirley Temple and many strangers would often stop and say how beautiful Colleen was.

Soon, after the birth of Colleen, Karen suffered with post natal depression which at the time was a surprise to both of us. Karen always wanted a girl and the birth of our daughter had been another blessing, yet it didn't stop Karen suffering with depression. At first, I didn't understand what was happening to Karen, she always seemed to be angry, and had no time for anything; her moods were variable which was unusual for her. This malaise went on for several months before I suggested to Karen to see a doctor and get some help, Karen was reluctant at first saying there was nothing wrong with her. But, I made her go realising that she definitely needed help I didn't realise how deadly post natal depression could be.

In the end Karen was glad I forced her to seek help, she didn't realise she needed help I guess that's symptomatic of the disorder. But at the back of our minds we had the constant worry of the nuclear threat. What would the world be like for our children; would it be worth living through all that hell? We even considered buying a shelter but we couldn't afford the cost we just didn't have the money.

Looking back now, the whole scenario was madness, we were better off dead. That's how we felt at the time, if it happened then we would just close our eyes and say our goodbyes, and hope it was quick.

We were drawn in to this fatalism. If the government was trying to frighten us with their propaganda then it worked, all our ambition we had for our family had gone. The TV programmes would tell us crazy things like put your head between your knees and position yourself under a table and hope for the best. A manic depressive's nightmare had begun; all you worried about was the future for your kids. You would see stories on TV how some people who could afford the cost had constructed purpose built shelters and stocked up for what appeared to be the future Armageddon.

I realised even then that you couldn't trust the governments, they tried to sell you their propaganda which seemed to me to be a bunch of lies about how to protect yourself with simple ideas like hiding under tables when we knew it would all be a waste of time.

If the threat was real the governments weren't spending any money on building shelters for the majority of the population. They were saying, fuck you and stick your head between your knees and that was that. We will probably never know what the government was really thinking until 50 years from now when secret classified documents are released under the Freedom of Information Act.

Karen and I and millions of other people lived through a period when we didn't think too much about today we worried if there would be a tomorrow. Through all these years I didn't think about ambition and with my manic depression I was lucky if a cared about living. It was real alright with pamphlets dropping through the letter box that insanely told you what to do, but you knew there was nothing you could do.

I can remember only having thoughts for Jamie and Colleen and feeling sad that they might not get to have a life. Karen and I would cry together and only worry about our children in a world that was totally insane. The politicians had gone mad as if it was a game, and the best they could offer us was to hold your head between your knees.

As the years passed and the kids grew I loved the times cuddled up with Jamie on one side and

Colleen on the other side watching TV. I would also tell stories and laugh and play with them, we would sometimes play a ticklish game where who would laugh first. These years are special to me and I wouldn't try to change them for anything. I love my children for they mean everything to me. Even though my depression was a constant problem this wouldn't stop me having time and loving my children.

Eventually, Karen and I decided to go to marriage guidance counselling to help save our marriage. After over two years of marriage guidance counselling, which did help us come to terms with many of the issues in our marriage, like why we never seemed to kiss and cuddle. It became clear that the problem was mainly me I had deep seated anxieties, which could only be resolved by having psychiatric help. It had been a journey of many years to come to this point.

Karen found it hard to understand, she was in a world far away from anything of that kind, but that wasn't her fault she had a normal childhood protected from the dangers of the world. The hardest thing that Karen wasn't able to do was to show me love with a hug it wasn't something she had inherited from her mother and she hadn't been close to her father in that way. She loved her father but just wasn't able to show it, and it was the same for me. But that is not her fault I was just someone that needed to be loved and shown that love.

Karen and I loved each other, but it was hard for us to show that love in a physical way, we just were not the type to be hugging and kissing all the time. I can't blame that on Karen, I was just the same. I don't think that I started to realise much of the problems between us were my fault until I started having counselling. I believe the counselling brought out the real me, the person I would have been if I hadn't been mentally abused as a child. I kept all this hidden from Karen until well into our marriage, it was almost 18 years before I started to talk about what had happened to me.

Most of the time Karen would assume I just suffered from bouts of depression that would come and go and didn't really understand why, and nor did I.

Karen had found it difficult at times living with me; the years of depression were a cycle of manic episodes where I would live in a world for months in a deep darkness, sometimes suicidal on a daily basis. Doctors, psychiatrists and drugs, nothing seemed to help. I would come to rely on self medication than on prescription drugs. Many years of counselling slowly started to help me come to terms with the mental abuse I had suffered as a child. But, it was a long journey for me so much had been buried.

The weekly counselling slowly started to unwind my twisted mind. I had kept so much hidden deep in my memory, that I had tried to forget what had happened to me, and at times I wondered if it really happened, but it had. It was just my way of dealing with the trauma in my childhood it was safer that way.

Over the years of counselling I would gradually come to terms with what had happened, even though at times I was reluctant to talk. It was difficult for me to trust anyone, it still is today. The journey had been long, and only with myself. It had taken a lot of courage to talk to strangers, people I didn't know if I could trust. It had taken many years before I said a single word to Karen who I could always trust. Yet, it was years later that I would break a trust we had together.

The most sacred trust that I broke between the two of us still pains me now, as it did then. I learnt a valuable lesson that the mistakes we make do not only hurt us but also the very people we love. I didn't set out to break the trust it just happened without me thinking about the consequences.

As the years passed I would rely on wacky backy to help me come to terms with my depression. Two and nine make twenty-nine, I was doing drugs at twenty-nine is from a lyric I wrote some years later about the years of drug abuse. I had started out late in life with the self medication, I guess you could say something I am not proud off, but I am just being honest and not condoning my actions in any way.

My wacky backy years were a release to the torment I felt, dealing with severe depression when the doctors appeared to fail me.

Puffing away on the wacky-backy I would spend many hours just listening to music and enjoying the sensation of feeling good inside. Essentially a non-smoker, having given up tobacco many years earlier it was strange to be puffing on a pipe.

Occasional, I would puff on my pipe to unwind the stress and strains of my melancholy; reaching sometimes a kind of peace, a place where I felt at home. I was consoling myself with the belief that what I was doing was natural; God had created these plants and they had been used for thousands of years by people's of ancient cultures to heal and evoke spirits.

I do not condone my actions in any way or want to preach about the rights and wrongs of smoking the ganja but let's face it even presidents have admitted smoking the occasional spliff. We can be hypocritical in our procrastinations and denials but the public are not stupid or green. I felt I had no choice, it was the only relief I felt from the black cloud that constantly lived as my shadow.

The doctors had failed me and at the time it was the only crutch I had. It got me through the years when nothing else was there for my depression. Admittedly, now, I can see it was the doctors who failed me. I had all this history of depression, yet they failed to join the dots and correctly diagnose me as bipolar.

Back then doctors and even some today do not understand manic depression; they view the symptoms as just a bout of everyday depression which many of us can suffer sometimes. The journey would be long and sometimes I did not even know where I was going.

It was now 1990, my father had returned from the States unexpectedly. At first he wouldn't talk about the reason, but finally through my persistence I found out that a long term relationship with an English girl in America had ended. He never gave the reason. The first couple of weeks I felt obliged to put him up in my home. I soon found out it was a poor decision. He would say things to the kids that Karen and I did not like, the same old shit he would say to me as a child. Although, it was a novelty to see my dad and have him literally on the door step I soon found a friend who could house him.

Over the years I got to know my dad the more I found I did not like him. Each year I felt obliged to invite him over for Christmas dinner, but each year he never showed. I never understood how he had more to say about other kids of friends he knew America, yet he never bothered with Colleen and Jamie. He was my dad, but most of the time I kept my distance. I failed to understand him. I tried to reconcile him with his mother but this also failed, it was a waste of time. I guess, I was looking for that happy family feeling I never had.

The many years of counselling were good for me, it had been a necessary road to recovery, but it also released a lot of anxiety in me. Maybe I had missed out on my teenage years, Karen and I had married young, and I had runaway from my life with a vindictive grandmother. I wasn't sure, the doubts inside were a constant strain on our marriage. It must have been hell for Karen sometimes I only hope she understood and forgave me some years later.

Near the end of our marriage I would break a trust. Sometimes I had to blame the counselling for releasing feelings maybe I had hidden inside for so long. But, that wasn't it, this just showed me how I was trying to hurt the very person I loved. I have heard the same said many times about how we end up hurting the very people we love, a kind of reaction to push the other person away. A kind of self-destruct mode where we end up hurting everyone we love.

At the time I was working as salesman and had wandered into a pub for a drink and something to eat when before I knew what was happening, the deceit was about to occur. I had slept with another woman. I can say I have only broken the golden rule once, and it pains me even now all these years later to talk about it. All I can say is this – don't do it.

When I think about what I did, even now and then, I can see all the pain it caused. People might want to ask, 'Was it worth it?' But it's not a case of whether it was worth it or not, that's not the point, I broke a sacred trust between two people that is the most important. And, no, it wasn't worth it.

I know that our marriage was coming to an end, but it was still wrong what I did. When two people aren't meant to be together there's always the right way to go about separating that relationship and the wrong way, I chose the wrong way. We all make mistakes and we have to learn from them, but it's just unfortunate that those mistakes don't just hurt us, they hurt others too.

When I told Karen, I wasn't prepared for all the pain I could see in her face. Maybe I shouldn't have told Karen, but I was wrecked with guilt, it was one of the lowest moments of my life. From that moment onwards I vowed to keep that scared trust again.

With my mind betwixt and I didn't know which way to go near the end of our marriage, I needed answers. When I would ask the counsellors for advice they explained they couldn't give that kind of advice. I understand that now but at the time I couldn't see why. When I did ask my dad about what to do about my marriage I was not expecting what he had to say. He said, 'Karen is a nice girl and mother and you'll find it hard to find another,' and this comment I couldn't believe coming from him. But, I guess he knew Karen had always been the same, someone you could always trust, and who never had a bad word to say about anyone. I think even my grandmother had the same feelings about Karen but just couldn't admit to it. She was glad in a way the day I said I had split with Karen. It was vindication of what she wanted from day one, that Karen wasn't good enough for me.

The day I left the home Karen and I had shared for so many years I will never forget it was one of the worst days of my life. I had packed a bag and was undecided at the bottom of the stairs whether to go or stay. I knew if I went, that would be the end of a marriage that had lasted over 22 years and if I stayed, would I be able to continue in a marriage I was unhappy with. I would miss the home life with Jamie and Colleen and being a family.

My heart and head were all over the place I felt sick in the stomach I didn't know what to do. I remember Jamie coming down the stairs and hearing Karen crying in the bedroom upstairs and Jamie saying, '*Just go dad.*' I looked him in the eyes. What he thought I wasn't sure. I turned around and went outside. With tears in my eyes I got in the car and left. I promised myself I would see Colleen and Jamie as much as I could. Over the following years I would have very close contact with my children, always available for them, still trying to lessen the pain that I had caused for us.

It's Never Too Late

Do You Believe in Miracles or Luck?

> *"If a man be lucky, there is no foretelling the possible extent of his good fortune. Pitch him into the Euphrates and like as not he will swim out with a pearl in his hand,"*
> *a* Babylonian Proverb

So what is luck? Some people believe that luck is nothing more than pure superstition with events happening outside their control. Based on an accident or chance event, luck can be seen to be a faith in a superstition, an unseen force.

The following account of what happened to me I will let you decide if I was lucky or not? But, keep in mind the words from the French author Georges Bernanos, he said, *"What we call chance might be the logic of God."*

After Karen and I had separated I was trying to re-live my youth again, by going to hedonist holiday destinations and having some overdue fun. I wanted to forget everything and just enjoy my new freedom. The only release was to re-live my youth again somehow, and forget the sadness I felt inside. Alone, I found myself on the Spanish island of Ibiza off the coast of Spain.

Ibiza was a European hotspot for drugs, booze and music. Ibiza was a Mecca for those who wanted to experience the nightlife of dance clubs and the party scene. The island from the early 1960s had been a haven of the flower power hippy revolution, subsequently it earned the cult status as the place where new music saw a grass roots following. In the 1970s and 1980s saw techno dance music explode on the scene and much of this early music started life on the island of Ibiza. I wanted to be a part of the music scene and somehow deal with the depression that had clouded my marriage.

Surrounded by beautiful warm blue sea you could lay on the beach all day and party all night, it was heaven. You could not help but fall in love with the island, hot days and cool nights, and everything was cheap except the clubs.

Mega size dance clubs were a party goers dream, some had capacities that ran into thousands. Every night I would get laced with a cocktail of alcohol and drugs. I just wanted to lose the black cloud of depression the constantly followed me. The music would send me into a trance and I was free again.

You didn't need Viagra to get excited the whole island oozed sex, the beaches were layered with topless girls it was a voyeur's paradise.

During the day the bars in St Antonio Bay where I was staying were just as full as the night time with people who had not stopped partying from the night before, it was just 24 hours.

Some days I would paint the scenery sitting under the shade of a palm tree. Listening to the sound of music playing where ever you went I would write down lyrics and try to compose a poem. I tried to forget the past and my marriage break-up. The beauty of the island inspired me to be creative at the same time I would be partying all night.

The place was a buzz with the sound of scooters as everyone who was anyone hired them to get around the island; it was manic with teenagers whizzing around like weasels on speed at times.

Then one day I decided to hire a scooter, thinking I needed to be part of the teenager scene. The trouble was I had never really ridden a scooter or motorbike before. But, it looked so easy, everyone else was riding scooters I figured why couldn't I. Before I say any more, please don't try this at home. The Spanish lady at the hire centre tried to explain what to do, it looked so easy but I didn't understand the lingo. She didn't mind that I didn't have insurance, she didn't ask, but that was the last of my worries.

Revving the scooter up on the boulevard she showed me how it worked and I got on the scooter ready to take to the streets. My hands grasped the handles and as I turned my hand the scooter just accelerated down the street heading for the main street where all the traffic and people were. I was terrified. The scooter was speeding down the street as if it had bolted like a horse out of stalls at a race track, and I couldn't stop it.

All I could think off was the traffic ahead, the parked cars and anyone that may walk by at any time. My face was in horror. Ahead of me was a parked car and I was heading straight for it, and over it and into the main traffic. I just couldn't stop the scooter; I didn't know what to do. All I could do is pray and ask God to save me and so I said, 'Please God save me.'

At that very second the scooter spun sideways and stopped within inches of hitting the parked car. I couldn't believe my eyes. It was a miracle how it happened and I will never forget. To this day I believe it was a miracle and not luck but I will let you decide.

Believe me, the danger I was in was horrific not just to me but also to any passing pedestrians. It was a miracle to me how that scooter stopped. As I sat there in shock reflecting on what had happened I prayed again, and thanked God for saving me.

What happened to me with the scooter was a miracle, not luck and definitely not chance. I believe luck and chance are two different observations we make. For one can have good luck only to lose it all foolishly, and then try to blame others when really its our greed that drives us to be reckless when fortune favours our shores. I believe luck can come your way the harder you work. Honest and hard work teaches us to appreciate our labour and our reward reminds us to be wise with what we earn.

Remember let hard work be your friend. Do not complain about your reward or how hard the work might be. Try to make the hard labour work for you as Thomas Jefferson said, *"I find that the harder I work the more luck I seem to have."* Often people will view luck in terms of gambling. Gambling is trying to take a shortcut and is neither productive nor rewarding.

For instance, think about punters at a casino, sometimes they win and sometimes they don't, but in the long run the casino comes out ahead. Nothing different here, this happens everyday in a casino some where, right? How do you think they built Las Vegas? What we are dealing with here is chance not luck. Chance is just an expression of the odds, and sometimes you beat the odds and end up winning.

Luck is different it's just an observation we make about an event. We all suffer bad luck of one form or another at some point, but it takes a strong person to keep going. Events in my life haven't always been easy and you could say I've been lucky to have had a strong personality to keep going.

I know that we can all experience a series of lucky and unlucky events occurring outside of our control. *"All of us have bad luck and good luck. The man who persists through the bad luck -- who keeps right on going -- is the man who is there when the good luck comes -- and is ready to receive it,"* by Robert Collier the prolific self-help author. Even in my darkest moments when I have felt like giving up, and there have been many of these, I have kept on going for my children.

Some of us think in the wrong way we let our self become subjected to negative thoughts, we self-destruct. You hear many people say, '*I never win anything*' or '*I'm just not lucky.*' My grandmother would always say '*I never win anything,*' and I don't think she did. This just illustrates the point that she just had a very negative mind set, which was more prominent after my grandfather died.

However, having bipolar has taught me to be positive and allow my mind to stay positive as much as possible. By doing this I believe you can alter your life, allowing positive events to occur. I believe you can change your luck at any time. And, "*The best luck of all is the luck you make for yourself*," by Douglas Macarthur.

We have talked about miracles which I believe we can all experience at some point in our lives. How if we stay positive and work harder we can change our luck.

How luck and chances in my view are different observations. Luck can be seen as a superstition, an unseen force, and chance an expression of the odds. Sometimes you win, sometimes you don't.

It's Never Too Late

Love is Everything

"A man in love mistakes a pimple for a dimple,"
a Japanese Proverb

Often, our mistakes haunt us for a very long time. I was exhausted with those mistakes. The previous two years separated from my wife I was a wreck with a cargo of doubt. It just happens you get married for whatever reason. I do not regret getting married we were blessed with two beautiful children. We were young and everyone encouraged us to get married. It's one of the greatest gifts you can receive, the blessing of children. Love, yes it can fade and maybe it seemed the right thing to do at the time. Sometimes in life we doubt ourselves not knowing whether what we do is right or wrong. One thing for sure, being bipolar, and understanding the characteristics of the disorder now makes me aware that sometimes we have a tendency to fall in and out of love like a revolving door. I only wish I had been diagnosed in my youth, but I wouldn't change anything I would still have married Karen.

I often envy other people's love that seems to endure and I long for the same feelings. I fell in love with Jane not long after getting divorced from the marriage of what seems a life time.

Actually, I had been married for over 22 years and for the most part happy. I first met Jane at one of those singles parties that lonely people seem to end up at especially when those teenage years are long gone, and it becomes increasingly more difficult to meet a suitable partner.

Don't get me wrong these single parties have there uses, after all, everyone there is looking for someone or that is what you think. I definitely needed someone I could love again. Loneliness is not something I would wish on anyone, it can tear your heart out.

Surveying the talent and the competition was the evening's entertainment and I was optimistic it would be a good night. I wasn't in a panic just yet that would come later maybe, if I didn't strike lucky.

It's a bit like a race where everyone is a runner, and you don't want to end up going home, after finishing last without the slightest hint of a future date. Each time it appears harder and takes longer to find new love. I have loved and lost. Will I ever find that one love that lasts I ask myself? Alfred Lord Tennyson said, *"Tis better to have loved and lost, than never to have loved at all."* Without having loved we are empty souls cast adrift without passion or emotion, a bare vessel as drifting flotsam. All these thoughts raced through my mind as my eyes surveyed the crowd. Would I find another Karen someone that I could love again without all the emotional baggage that I had brought to the table?

Introducing myself to a group of people I didn't know I sat down, and got stuck into the mountain of food available as we all munched away on the potato chips, pastry rolls, quiche, sandwiches, and other tasty goodies, when one of the organisers of the singles party asked me who I was. He was a short and skinny man. Politely, I told him, and explained that a member of the singles group had invited me so I could take a look and see if I wanted to join the group. There is always someone that wants to spoil the party, I was thinking.

The guy saw me as a threat, as more competition, I don't know but I suspect it was the case. He was quite rude saying I should have been a paid up member of the singles group before coming to the party. I had a feeling if I had been a woman he would have not mentioned a word, and been glad I had turned up because from what I could see he needed all the help he could get. Feeling threatened and alone with this attack I was thinking: *All I wanted was a good night out.*

Anyway, I said to him, *'usually when I buy a pair of shoes, I like to try them on first,'* whereupon he didn't say another word. Hey! I been invited by one of the members of the singles group to a party, I wasn't expecting the guy to get down my throat. I just wanted to have some fun and maybe find a suitable date if I got lucky. Passive is my name. I do not look for trouble just the opposite.

Why is it short guys with a little power suddenly become little Hitler's strutting around like headless chickens. It's a bit like those individuals who strut around talking on their cell phones acting like some sort of mini-celebrity as they start to have a conversation at decibels above everyone else. As if they needed to announce on their phones to the world that they're some how important, don't you find that annoying behaviour, I just hope I don't act like that.

Anyway, I think everyone at the table could see the fun in what I had said, because they were all eager to find out more about me, Jane in particular.

Jane was curious to know more about my art work as I had explained to her that one of my passions was to paint. Jane was interesting too; she had never married, but had travelled the world working in some exotic locations, and by all accounts had done some interesting jobs. She told me as a security officer she had worked in Jamaica, and had to use her gun on several occasions. She explained that drugs and street gangs were a major problem, and many companies employed security officers.

Meeting a woman for the first time in my life that carried a gun for a living was a new experience for me. Here was a beautiful blond, with deep blue eyes with a generous rounded curvaceous figure, who I would have never imagined daily had been risking her life. I quickly got round to inviting Jane and a friend to my apartment to view some of my art work the following week.

It wasn't long before Jane and I were dating, though, at first she was hesitant stating she wasn't into long term relationships. In a way I understood this as maybe it was a consequence of never being married before, and moving around the world.

The strange thing was as soon as I started to fall in love with her she got cold feet and looking back I can see why, though at the time I didn't understand her reasons. I guess my mind was so clouded by my love for her that I just couldn't see it her way. Maybe these aren't the right words to describe the feeling but sometimes we feel lost, like an empty shell on a beach.

Love is difficult to find yet we doubt ourselves when we find it. I know I do, more like a doubting Thomas that refuses to believe that love has found its shadow.

We had many things in common, the love of art, the passion of nature and the thrill of feeling young again. We would go for walks in the countryside and have picnics and talk about the books that we had read. It all appeared rosy and I felt that Jane was the girl for me.

Then it hit me like a brick wall, stopped me dead in my tracks when she phoned one day to tell me not to bother coming over later to see her as we had planned. Jane explained quietly that she wasn't in love with me. I just couldn't believe what she was telling me, we hadn't had any arguments in all the time we had been together. In fact, it seemed we were made for each other; everything had been great between us. The tears started to well up in my eyes, ready to cascade in a flurry when I asked her why she could not say this to my face, it was gutless. I could hear the sadness in her voice and almost feel the tears.

The honeymoon period was over. Jane had made it plain our love was over. I hate that part in relationships, when everything appears great, you forget you need eye glasses; you fail to see all the flaws as if you've been walking around in a dense fog. It must be the emotion of new love that clouds your vision almost as if you're wearing steamy goggles, and not much else except maybe you're in top speed arousal mode.

I don't know about you but love does have its way of grabbing you by the throat and not letting go until you've been tamed. Jane had tamed me and was willing to let me go.

How long does the honeymoon period usually last? It's a simple question. When does the love fade as many couples discover in a relatively short period? I find this period doesn't last that long usually only a few weeks or months before we sink into the abyss. We expect it to last but more often than not the honeymoon period disappears like a ship in the Bermuda triangle. Between Jane and me it lasted only a couple months before it was gone forever.

She agreed to see me some time later when we spent the day together on a shopping escapade. Jane told me she couldn't continue with the relationship because she was falling in love with me. She didn't want that to happen, it was something that experience had taught her to avoid. Jane had never been married before. The risk of being hurt was too big and she knew that it hadn't been long since my divorce, and that I also wasn't ready for another long term relationship.

In a way she was right, but it still hurt me as if all the emotion had been drained from me; I felt as if I had boots on but no laces. There're no easy answers, I wish there were in the game of love. The lovers will entangle until they choose to disentangle. Sex doesn't last long but love well that's a different feeling and should last a lot longer.

We had sex that day. Jane wanted it more than I did and it was more lust than love, all my feelings appeared to have vanished that day. Love is the greatest gift we can have and give. We should always seek to love rather than hate. I didn't hate Jane or the reasons why she could not fall in love with me. The more we love the better the world will be to live in.

Sometimes I would wish I had someone I can love with, cry and laugh. I would ask myself is that too much to want? I had fallen in love with Jane even though it didn't last.

Looking back I would say love comes and goes and you never really know what the other partner is thinking. One thing is for sure; beware of chain smoking nurses because I went from a non smoker to a cigar smoker faster than you can say Jack shit. It's the stress of being a nurse that Jane couldn't handle or just the risk of falling in love I guess.

They say that at some point in life you meet your equal, your soul mate. I can't say that I have. Until maybe sometime later when after many years I can reflect, and say, yes you do meet your soul mate eventually. We want the love of our partners; our children, parents, friends and family but the love from our partners is sometimes like a child that craves a new toy, we play with it until it becomes too familiar. Yet, without love we are lost in this world where the greatest gift we can give or receive is love. Jane was frightened to give that love and let it go.

Life is a rollercoaster, sometimes you are ahead and sometimes not. Finding love can be a mirage that appears and disappears just as quickly, its part of the fun I guess. Yet you need to understand that people with bipolar have extreme sexual desires that ride a cloud so high sometimes we don't know what our true feelings are. It's difficult for us, its part of our make up. We can fall in and out of love just as easy as baking a cake. Don't get me wrong it's not our choice, but because of our character for some reason we are not stable, but then who is when it comes to love. But then love is everything.

Confidence Lets Talk

"If you want to achieve things in life, you've just got to do them, and if you're talented and smart, you'll succeed."
by Juliana Hatfield

Many of us lack confidence at different times in our lives. Some of us will say, *'I totally lack confidence.'* They are like egomaniacs they blow everything out of proportion as if they're living under a microscope. Confidence can come and go just like the focus of a microscope.

Having bipolar has helped me build my self-confidence over the years by using strategies that I have had to use to force myself to get well again. By attempting new tasks regardless of whether I succeed or fail I am using a strategy for future success. Also, by learning to accept that I have this disorder I have gained the confidence to deal with life. I can't remove the condition but I can change the way I think about it.

On any road to recovery it's always hard, but once you make the first step the following journey is less. Confucius said, "*A journey of a thousand miles begins with a single step.*"

Many new things in my life I have tried and I haven't always been good at all of them or even liked doing them. Shortly after my divorce I attempted activities that I thought might help with my depression. Activities that would get me out of the apartment and help me socialise more. There is nothing worse than being a social leper. You become a hermit without realising what's happening to you. I was also becoming a couch potato and needed to lose some weight. I had tried jogging years before and found personally that it was too boring, and I had done the gym routine for several years and wasn't ready to go back to that ball breaker. You have to learn to be confident to succeed in what you want to achieve.

There are many times in our lives when we feel less confident with our ability to cope, this is usually more to do with fear of failure than the lack of confidence. We all want to be that person who we imagine has that confidence in any scenario, being able to socialise, at that job interview, chatting up girls or boys and just being able to handle anything that comes our way. We all wish we could be a more confident person which would help us in our everyday lives. We don't want to be that person in the corner hiding, we want to be at the front of the class ready and confident to put our hands up not worried what people may think, and just want to be free to be happy about who we are. And, that was what I was about to do, get out of that corner and starting fighting my depression. I wasn't ready to give up I still had a few more rounds left in me.

I decided to enrol at the local sports hall and start evening yoga classes. Fearing that I was too fat and I wouldn't be able to get my body into impossible positions I almost didn't get to the Yoga classes preferring the comfortable couch position.

However, almost the fear of being to fat and what people may think nearly stopped me trying Yoga, and I would have missed so much. But I did go and got my fat butt down the sports hall and was amazed to find I really enjoyed myself. Once I got over the fear that everyone would be looking at me, which wasn't the case I soon started to relax. It did beat staring at that television for endless hours, and of course I got to meet some interesting women but that wasn't my primary motive. As the weeks and months went by I learnt so much about my body I started to lose weight without even thinking about it.

My confidence grew and I was amazed at how I could contort my body into all sorts of weird and wonderful positions. One added bonus was I learnt the art of meditation, which later would become another strategy I would use to combat my constant depression.

I found that its important to learn self-belief whether one succeeds or not in something we attempt. Part of learning self-confidence is the ability to try, it's not about the eventual outcome, more important is our demeanour not worrying about what people may think and just enjoying ourselves. I was using this strategy primarily to deal with my depression but at the same time my confidence was growing.

Confidence I found was a skill and just like any other can be taught and mastered. If you are wondering at this moment whether you should go on to higher education, try for that better job, or ask that girl or boy out for a date and questioning yourself with the nagging doubt *will it be worth it.* Ask yourself this question - Am I doing it for me? What I am trying to address here is many people do things not for themselves but because they feel expected to from parents or friends. Challenge yourself for you not someone else. I began to challenge myself and at the same time able to conquer my fears.

Amazed at how my confidence had improved since I got myself off that couch and started Yoga, I began to look for other challenges. I read a local newspaper article one day about a film director who was planning to shoot some of his film in the locality. The article explained that the director would be requiring extras and doubles for some of the scenes. I decided to write to the director explaining that I had done some amateur dramatics and that I would like to audition if that was possible.

My confidence had grown but I wasn't arrogant about my chances of obtaining an audition. Being self-confident is not about an indifference to the world around you, having a blasé attitude as if nothing matters but you. If you stick your head in the sand in the belief that you are always right and everyone else is wrong, it's more likely you'll have difficulty coping and your apparent self-confidence is a mirage of sand built on arrogance. Even when I found my confidence growing I kept myself grounded.

Going around with an air of superiority and not realistically being able to evaluate the needs of others is often a sign that you're heading towards a disaster. This is similar to what I experience when I'm in a manic phase of my bipolar disorder, something I am aware of now but not at this time. It's also a characteristic you see often in people who suddenly are given some authority, you know, the office boss, the traffic warden, and such like, the little Hitler's.

Sure enough, I got a reply explaining the date, time and location of the auditions. This was great, I thought, but the auditions also coincided with a yoga festival that I wanted to attend the same day. So I phoned and explained my situation with the director's secretary and I asked if I could go first as apparently there would be around 300 people attending auditions that day. Sure enough, that's what happened; I was one of the first to get in front of those rolling cameras, just as well because the queue seemed at least a mile long.

Anyway, I had practiced reciting some Shakespeare for days, just in case they asked me to recite something to test my voice. I wasn't sure what the procedure would be, I had never been to a real audition before, and I was in another world as far as professional acting goes.

The first thing the director did was tell me briefly what the film was about and handed me a script and told me my part. From memory, I think the film was called 'My Darling Tom,' so there I was, trying to act the part of a terrorist from a few lines while the cameras rolled. Talk about being nervous. I was terrified and I failed, but in many ways I enjoyed the experience and my recital of Shakespeare '*to be or not to be*' was definitely not to be, I missed so many key words I went from word perfect to don't bother.

The key to achieving self-confidence is therefore a recognition that all the activities we attempt might not turn out to be successful, and that we should not dwell on negative results. Success comes to those that keep trying, and self-confidence maintains our enjoyment until we reach our goals. Although my recital of Shakespeare was a failure, I didn't let it get me down. I wasn't expecting to become the next Sir Laurence Olivier.

Self-belief allows us to cope in any situation with the ability to manage failure as part of the road to a successful outcome. An athlete may compete in many events and only win a few, its part of the journey.

At the end when I analysed myself I said, '*I was glad that I had challenged myself and that I'd also enjoyed the experience of the audition.*' For getting up there and having a go I gave myself ten out ten and then went on to enjoy the rest of the day at the yoga festival.

So don't fear failure, just challenge yourself and don't worry about what other people may think, and don't be too critical of your performance. Give yourself a pat on the back for trying, and keep building that confidence.

After each challenge self-evaluate and if you can, ask a friend about how they thought you performed. Again, don't worry if they criticise or praise your efforts. If they criticise your efforts, look to see if it was justified, and how maybe you could improve next time. Be positive whatever the outcome, remembering to take the good and bad comments constructively. Praise yourself for trying.

The importance of self analysis is more vital than what your friends may have to say. The first step in confidence building is to overcome fear of failure and also the criticism that might come from your efforts. The second point here is that although criticism is often bias you can also learn to take the good from the bad and therefore improve your confidence or skill.

Confidence is not something you are born with, you learn and grow and as a child your parents should encourage confidence in you by praising things you do well. You can teach yourself to be confident. By praising yourself each time we do things well and knowing that we did our best and that our best is good enough, we can learn self-confidence.

The level of confidence can also change dependent on our moods, sometimes we feel good so naturally our confidence is good and when we feel down or depressed our confidence can hit rock bottom. So confidence is not a characteristic that is built into our personalities.

Being bipolar, I always remember to test my mood knowing that when I am in a black mood my confidence will not be at its best. It's something that I am aware of so I can make allowance for it in what I am planning to do. I try to remind myself about the things I have tried and achieved to bring myself out of the black depression that I call my black cloud.

So, I would say give it a go, try new things, do not be afraid of what people may think and build your confidence. Even if some days you may feel you have lost your confidence, I believe this is only a temporary blimp.

You can always think about the things you have tried, and your inner confidence will return. Learn to praise other people; this will also help to build your self-belief. I challenged myself, can you?

Chasing the Circle Equals Never Being Satisfied

"Who so loves believes the impossible,"
by Elizabeth Barrett Browning

Should we be satisfied with each other, continually want more, or is it just a hopeless cause? Can we satisfy each other enough even when we always appear to want more? One day you wake up where you started and you're still not satisfied. This happened to me but I knew it was my fault. Have you ever been there, do you know what I mean?

It was the summer 0f 2003 and I had been chasing the circle for several years now. I had been dating Jill for about 3 years, sometimes happy and sometimes not. I had met Jill briefly one night about 11 years before at a party when I was still married to Karen. Looking back it was like an invisible leash had been pulling me in one direction or another.

Remembering the funny words that Groucho Marx said, *"Man does not control his own fate. The women in his life do that for him,"* which isn't that far from the truth, especially in retrospect concerning what happened to me. Karen and I had gone to our neighbour Julie's party, which was a change for us because we didn't get out much with a young daughter and son to look after. I remember walking into Julie's lounge and all I could see was a crowd of people, most of whom I didn't know. It was the typical home party where some were sitting and most were standing, trying to mingle with people you didn't know.

As I first I caught sight of Jill in all that radiate light I felt an immediate attraction. She had that cheeky, well-modelled face and blond shoulder length hair, those looks that would want to make you say, *'wow!'* When our eyes connected she hypnotized me with that sensuous cute smile, similar to that of a *miss world's* model.

And I guess I was hooked from that moment on; she caught me there and then, my heart was pumping hard, I could feel the butterflies in my stomach eager to meet hers. My body tingled, ready to hold this perfect ten, an angel of beauty with no exaggeration, a princess among women. It was no surprise to see she had a man that clung to her like a mole.

My wife and I were packed in with other revellers at the party; you could just about hear yourself speak above the pop music that was blasting out. And, I know what you're thinking but I am being honest; I am writing a true story. Criticise me yes, but wait at least until the end.

I grabbed a beer and attempted to mingle, but all I could see in the corner was a girl who looked like a Venus and some other mortal that shadowed her. I was thinking: *Lucky guy............she was hooked up, but not with me.* Envy and jealousy poured from me, I was envious of the guy, and jealous she wasn't holding my hand. I knew it was wrong to be thinking like that, I was married and that was that. But, occasionally our eyes would meet across the crowded room and I knew there was an instant attraction between us. In that sweet perfume that lingers I could sense that lure of attraction. *The attraction I had, was it beer goggles?* I thought for a moment. No. There was definitely an attraction on both sides. I was married with two young children so I wasn't about to jeopardise that for any women, even if she was a Venus. I just grabbed a beer satisfied my libido had been massaged, and carried on enjoying the party.

Later on I was introduced to Jill and her boyfriend by my wife; they were friends apparently, as our children went to the same school as Jill's.

Anyway, sometime later at the party I had to wander upstairs to relieve the pressure on my bladder, and being a man with a few drinks in his belly I didn't think to shut the door. Well, you can guess what happened next? I heard a sexy giggle behind me, as I turned my head it was Jill, the girl I couldn't keep my eyes off, my Venus with those shiny green eyes which looked deep into my heart. With slight embarrassment I smiled and said a few words, shyness preventing me saying what I was really feeling. Even though we didn't really know each other I could feel a physical attraction between us, but I left it there, I was married even if she wasn't.

Over the weeks and years that passed my wife would occasionally mention Jill, but to me it was someone my wife knew and that was all. Sometimes I would think about Jill and wonder what never was. Even living in the same small town I never saw Jill again, until one day about 8 years and a divorce later.

Strange how fate plays its part even if it takes a long time to play its hand. Meeting Jill in the same local supermarket that I had been shopping in for years, and had never once caught sight of her there, was weird. A rush of excitement took over me, she giggled and I smiled and we made a date to meet. She had not changed in those 8 years; she was still my dream girl.

Over the moon with happiness, I couldn't wait to hold her hand and feel that rush of emotions with that first kiss. Jealousy overcame me. I wanted to protect and forever hold her in my arms; I had wanted for this moment for so long.

When six months later Jill told me she wasn't in love with me, I was devastated. I had been so happy that some days I would sing my heart out with love on my way home from work.

In the end we stayed together, me more as a councillor for her problems than a lover sometimes. Jill would arrive home from work in tears and I would waste the weekend consoling her about the job, children and the previous marriage that was troubling her.

Late one night I found Jill on the floor of my apartment, she had taken an overdose of pills and I quickly called an ambulance. If I hadn't rung 999 she wouldn't have lived past that day.

Throughout these sad times I was still in love, I wanted to help Jill. So I supported her through the serious difficulties she was having, even when she told me that she was still in love with a former boyfriend that had raped her. I just could not believe what she had told me.

I couldn't believe it and was upset for her; she'd been raped and didn't want to go to the police. Jill was still in love with this jackal of a boyfriend who for several years never took her out, but just used her. Jill told me the jackal would come around at weekends and only when it suited him, as he was a married man.

From my perspective I was angry, and wanted to land one right on the jackal's chin. So in a way it isn't surprising looking back now, that I started to look elsewhere.

I started looking at other women and not feeling satisfied with Jill. And, looking back and analysing my actions, I was wrong to be eyeing up other women. Well, what would you do? Sure, I looked around but I never went astray. That is what I call - *chasing the circle*.

Not being satisfied because you're chasing something that you already have. We have to learn to be satisfied, we are born with what we have, yet some of us are not satisfied with what we are. There are blondes who want to be brunettes; men who want to be women. And on it goes, constant circles of dissatisfaction with who we are and want we want. We seek perfection but it is not possible, a mistaken ideal. Possibly an inherited fault, maybe a faulty gene or some other biological chemical imbalance that makes us want to be perfect.

Strife for perfection destroys who we are; imperfect souls cast adrift in the universe, which also isn't perfect, an indiscriminate chaos. All of us want to be someone different and some of us will pay lots of money to transform the way we look, a visit to the plastic surgeon has become as common a trip as to the dentist.

Mind you for a trip to the dentist these days you almost need to re-mortgage your home. I can understand that getting your beauty sleep is important for how you look but people who want to, for example, change the shape of their nose they've had since birth, should be happy with what they've got.

It took 8 years for fate to bring Jill and me together. Remember how I was full of happiness when I was dating Jill. Life is what you make it and I fucked up. Now I have had time to think about my life and how sometimes what you wish for does actually come true.

Can we hold on to what we find before it's washed away and just another memorable experience? I have learnt that, if you find what you're looking for, then believe this - don't get into that circle, chasing your tail. True happiness comes along only a few times and maybe just the once. But hey! Who gives a shit, right?

Sure, I have had a few relationships, but I am no Casanova, all this time I have been looking for love. Is that too much to ask? Difficult to find you might agree and that is probably why internet matchmaking sites are such big business. A day without love is a day lost, in my book.

Over the years my wisdom has grown and hopefully it has taught me some lessons from my experience, or perhaps not when I look back at all the fuckups I have made. We should all cherish wisdom, although at times I do not think I have any. If I had the Wisdom of Solomon I would not have as many wives as him, I would not be able to afford it. One divorce is painful enough, emotionally and financially. It was enough to end up a nervous wreck living in that poor house. Chasing the circle I realised, is never being satisfied.

Jill and I stayed together for about 3 years; I guess I should explain what happened. It was my fault, I can see that now, but at the time all I could see was just me. Looking back I think I was selfish, only thinking about what I wanted and not considering Jill's needs.

Our relationship finally split when I wanted to do a Masters degree, which meant moving to the other end of the country and Jill didn't want to move. Jill was settled with a new job and new friends, she didn't want to start again I couldn't blame her for that. Sure, we kept in touch for a few months but it wasn't long before Jill rang to tell me she had met someone else. We met up a few months later at Christmas. It was more a final goodbye, which I think hurt us both as we held hands and kissed and said goodbye.

Of course I was devastated and sad but I knew it was coming; you can't live a long distance apart, especially with any real commitment to each other, before one of you ends up meeting someone else. In my heart I still loved Jill, but I lost her by chasing the circle. So be careful what you wish for; your wishes can come true. They might take time, but they do happen eventually.

Opportunity Knocked at My Door

"Opportunities multiply as they are seized,"
by Sun Tzu

So let me tell you about the opportunity that knocked at my door.

When I had just gained my BSc Honours degree and was ready to start a new career in the summer of 2003, the opportunities seemed plenty for me to explore, even though I had been a late starter.

My time at university had been a journey of several years at first working towards gaining my first degree in computing. I had no idea about continuing on at university and doing further studies, for one thing I was in debt, and could not afford the fees for another degree.

Admittedly, I did really enjoy my time at university even though I was a mature student and nearly everyone around me was half my age. I soon made friends and became familiar with the on campus student union bar, where several nights a week I would enjoy getting a few drinks down my neck.

Nearing the end of my studies I did attend some seminars about post graduate courses available – more out of interest than any real commitment to carry on at university. Instead, I was chasing employment and the chance to get that high paid job in computing. But for some reason a master's degree in a computing related subject was still something that lingered on my mind.

My thoughts ranged from, 'would I be capable of doing a masters in computing, after all it was hard enough these past years at university studying computing at under graduate level' to 'did I need further pressure' and 'how would I afford the fees and also feed myself for another year and half?' I was already in enough debt and wasn't sure what help would be available or even if I could afford to borrow more money.

Something was nagging at me – was I good enough to be a computer professional? I wasn't sure. I didn't have many options. I looked into the costs of doing a master, the more I found out the less likely it was going to happen, as I couldn't borrow any more money.

The fact is, I put the idea about a master's degree on the back shelf – I thought that I might do it one day but for now I started looking for a job. While looking for jobs at the local career centre, conveniently located on the university campus, I stumbled upon some career brochures from other universities. It wasn't until I was reading one of these brochures that I noticed, purely by chance, an advert showing available master's degrees at a university way up north of where I was currently living.

This university was advertising the chance to do a masters degree with free funding with no fees , I couldn't believe it – yet, when I spoke to someone at the career centre they never mentioned this opportunity – so much for relying on so called career advisors – they didn't know shit as far as I was concerned.

Amazed that sometimes relying on other people is not always the best policy, and it just goes to show that doing your own foot work can sometimes pay off even though it might mean a hard slog. I rang the university that day to see if places were still available, and to find out more about applying for the bursary – and sure enough I was eligible and two months later I found myself doing a master's in Software Engineering in Artificial Intelligence.

What seemed an impossible proposition only a few months before, because I didn't have the money to pay for a master's degree, became a reality solely by my efforts of opening doors and looking for new opportunities, to me that is success?

And again I would say don't let these doors close on you when you receive setbacks. In the many books that I have read about influential people they often state how to overcome adversities by looking at the potential opportunities that often appear at the same time. It is those who come and look beyond the trees that can grasp hold of these moments as real opportunities, to make the best out of the up and downs of life.

It's Never Too Late

I Didn't Believe in Taking Shortcuts

"When it comes to success, there are no shortcuts,"
by Bo Bennett

It was nearing the end of 2003 and I was about to start a masters in Software Engineering in Artificial Intelligence at Sunderland University. It had been a long, tiring, eleven hour drive from Plymouth with everything I owned stuffed to the roof of my faithful old Citroen AX.

Arriving on the post graduate campus late in the evening with the prospect of unloading all my junk I was tired, but glad to have made it to Sunderland without breaking down along the way. My car had never been this far before and I wasn't sure it would make it. But, I had made it, and Sunderland would be my home for at least the next year and half. What happened after that I didn't know, or even care?

My room on the campus was on the ground floor which was lucky; it saved me lugging all my stuff up countless floors of an apartment block. There was a shared kitchen and lounge and my room had its own bathroom for those times when you needed to get in there quick. The campus had all the usual facilities including the student union bar, which was literally only a couple minutes walk away for me.

The first few days were the usual mayhem of not knowing where to go, but I soon made friends and found my way around the university campus. I had my initial doubts about the course and maybe I had bitten off more than I could chew. But I had made my bed, and it was a case of stick with it or just flunk out. The later just wasn't an option; I was broke and living off the university bursary. I had to succeed.

Soon, I was voted by most of the engineers to represent them as their student representative. It wasn't a job I particularly wanted but nearly everyone thought a mature candidate was the best choice, even the tutors who encouraged me to enter the election thought the same. My thoughts were: *Being a student representative meant a whole lot more work with the modest time I had to spare. I was doing a master that was challenging enough. What have I got myself into Stanley?*

It turned out to be a Godsend, you will see why later. Although at the time I didn't see it that way. It was also the starting point of a book that I would write about university life. Learning to turn what looked like a negative into a positive opportunity is one of the reasons I wanted to write this book.

My friends were crazy and I had a job keeping up with them on the nights we spent exploring Sunderland. They would drink more than I could and I guess it was all that youthful energy and being away from home that brought the devil out in them.

There were nights when we would return to the campus and carry on drinking until the sun came up the next morning. It was all good fun, but we had plenty of work to keep us tame and labouring over the keyboard. It was just as well I didn't want to end up becoming a student alcoholic.

I soon joined the university salsa club and some other local clubs to get away from the relentless boredom of my room. It wasn't long before I met with a Newcastle lass on the dance floor. I needed outside distractions to allay the stress of writing code and reading books all day.

Gill was a nice girl living in Newcastle about a half hours drive from Sunderland. I would go to the Tiger club in Newcastle once a week and salsa the night away. Gill could move across the dance floor and attract a lot of attention from the males as her blond hair and her slim firm body stirred their emotions. The first time I stayed at her place she drove all the way over to Sunderland to pick me up from the campus late one night. I told her the only way I could see her that night was if she could pick me up. She was over in a flash. That is what I call commitment.

As the weeks and months passed I could feel the stress slowly creeping up on me as the finishing line got ever closer. Each assignment passed and as I did each module the task appeared to get even harder. Just as well that I had Gill and the salsa club.

As the final exams drew closer with only a couple months to go the pressure mounted. I spent less time in the student union bar and unfortunately less time with Gill.

Several days had passed, and I had been locked away in my room struggling and juggling with computer problems, exam preparation and assignments and time was running out.

So far I had a record of all A's and B's, and was working towards a first in my masters degree and I didn't want to fuck up at the final hurdle. It had been hard work and no easy ride, these last few months.

The stress was manic; I knew I couldn't afford to fail. I was broke just living off the bursary, literally. There was no second chance for me; I couldn't afford to retake anything, not even a semester, a single assignment or module, absolutely sod all.

On top of all that I had a girlfriend, who was more manic than me. One minute she was phoning to say she wanted to finish with me, and I replied, "*That's Ok. I haven't got the time anyway.*" Two hours later she phones back to say she had been a bit hasty and now wanted to still continue with the relationship. It was bad enough that I had a computer that was just like a complaining wife that never stops nagging to update it self.

So there I was withdrawing into my interior world, trying to cope with no hope of a fairy godmother coming to my rescue.

Computer code would not run on my box. Although it ran fine on the campus boxes, I could not test my code and I was using up precious time. I even explained to the tutor my problems, he told me not to worry and just submit my work. Well, that is what I did in the end, I didn't believe in taking shortcuts as I call them.

My friend had suggested taking code from the internet, plagiarism, cheating, whatever you want to call it. That is what he was going to do. I told him not to do it but he went ahead anyway. He got caught and failed the module. Even in my darkest moments when I was thinking of failure I wasn't prepared to take shortcuts to success, especially if that meant cheating or stealing or whatever you want to call it.

So if I can do it then so can you. We all suffer with setbacks along the way but its part of the journey, a bit of a roller-coaster ride. I had worked hard academically, even though it was late in my life, and in some ways more difficult being a mature student. I was just a man, not superman. There was no magic power, no magic wand. As a mature student, I stretched myself to achieve what I wanted to achieve.

Even when thinking I was going to fail, I did not give up. Somehow, I found the strength to carry on in my effort to get a first in a master's degree. I didn't quite get there –not a first but I passed and went pretty close to getting a first, only just missing by two percent. I was not disappointed I had passed with flying colours, and in the end it didn't matter to me that I had not achieved a first. What was more important was that I had challenged myself by doing a master in a subject that was extremely testing.

Sure it was testing when I was up to my eyeballs in doubt, and I had students crying to me about their problems. Problems like the time when one of the university servers was more down more often than up right in the middle of exams preparation, and I had an assignment due in the following Friday. I successfully championed an extension of three days for the offending assignment even though the tutor wasn't a happy bunny, but he could see the sense. That gave many students including me enough time to hand in the assignment fully tested on the server. Even with this and other issues I found the time to help others although all I felt like doing was crawling into a corner and hiding. When that black cloud of depression struck me like lightning.

And the Godsend, well, that was when, as a student rep attending academic board meetings, I found out how important critical thinking was to passing a masters'. This was something with which I was able to inform all the students I represented. I am certain it saved my bacon and many others too.

It's Never Too Late

Bipolar Thinking – Critical Thinking

"The man who makes no mistakes does not usually make anything,"
by Theodore Roosevelt

Critical thinking would play a major part in my thinking over the following years. It was the summer of 2004 and I was in the midst of writing my dissertation. I had survived the gruelling months before by the skin of my teeth. If I had doubts then, I now had the tremendous task of submitting a dissertation for the masters.

I had learnt a lot as a student rep helping other students. Learning to cope when the situation got tough made me think more about what I was doing. I had found out about the importance of critical thinking, not just in an academic way. In my view it's similar to what I came to describe as bipolar thinking - learning to analyse opposing views. Hey, when you've had as much therapy as I've had you become an expert in self analysis. It made me think how you can often have a polarised view without any real truth to back it up.

I remembered what my grandmother would often say when she heard an Irish person on the TV. Her famous words were, *'I don't like the Irish.'* Whenever I questioned her why she didn't like the Irish I never got a straight answer. I don't think she really knew, maybe it was something she heard her parents say while growing up or some past event that she could not remember anymore that clouded her judgement.

Possibly, a single event that had harmed her in some way, and she had blackened every Irish person with the same brush since, I wasn't sure. Either way I knew it was wrong to let our bigotry and bias get in the way of us making informed decisions, and it was important to understand this in my street philosophy to live a better life.

Critical thinking and evaluation is a skill we can all learn to master which can help us have a balanced and informed view of life by making fewer assumptions based on our bias. Unfortunate as it is, it's often our mistakes that show us the path we must follow.

Anyway, don't fall in to the same trap as many students do at university; and get caught, hook, line and sinker into believing you know what critical thinking is only to find out you don't know. It reminds me of the quote by Albert Einstein, "*a little knowledge is a dangerous thing. So is a lot.*"

First, what is critical thinking? As many of us get confused as to what it really means. Critical thinking is about evaluating an argument without allowing your beliefs or bias to influence your reasoning whether to support or criticise the argument.

This reminds me of the time only a few months before when critical thinking would raise its head. At university I made friends with a Greek girl called Kiki who was studying for a MBA. It was great that Sunderland University provided their own buses for the post graduate students on campus. You didn't have to freeze your butt off walking to university. Sunderland being not far from bonny Scotland which was one of the coldest places you could live.

One day while on the bus to university I got talking to Kiki about her course and she explained how it was going. I asked her to tell me what was the most important aspect in business in a *word* or *sentence*. It wasn't meant to be a trick question. I just wanted to see want Kiki would say. She thought for a moment, and then went on to rattle off several sentences about this and that. To be fair, I don't think Kiki had thought for long enough, and don't forget I had spent more time thinking than she did about the question.

Besides, the question asked for one word or sentence, not a series of sentences. We can all fall into the trap of not listening and not thinking about what exactly the question asked. I told her the most important thing in business is *people* in my opinion; because it doesn't matter how well the product or service you're selling, *it's the people that matter.* If you have people that are unhappy and can't communicate, well, then your business is ultimately doomed.

Sure, there are a multitude of other important aspects, but I had asked for one word or sentence. That is where critical thinking can play its part in understanding what is really being asked. Sure, there's a bit more to critical thinking and evaluation but understanding the question is more important.

Let's face it, we all do it, we get on our soapbox and blast away without first evaluating our argument. It's an easy trap to fall into, to hold a particular belief and then support a similar belief without first evaluating the supporting evidence.

Critical thinking or evaluation is the ability to analyse and evaluate the work of others. Kiki had done this part okay, but had forgotten what the question had asked.

The reasoning and argument presented by the author must be well structured with supporting argument and evidence. Again, Kiki had done this part, but had forgotten what the question asked. Our ability to use the arguments of other people's work; whether its a written work, a piece of music ,an art work or any other original creative idea or thought, to present their argument or reasons for supporting a view is the art of critical thinking, but we must not forget to understand the question.

So now you know what it's all about? Well, it's never that simple there's a bit more meat on the bone, we all have that bias that I talked about earlier to deal with.

While I was at college, it was early on in my education that I got a severe shock to my senses. It's an important story so I hope you don't mind. I was the quiet type ready to listen to just about anyone. That was the problem, but I didn't know it then. I don't think I have changed much.

Anyway, college back then was a new haven, you got to meet new friends; I enjoyed the lifestyle – beer, girls, and the nightlife, but hated the work. But, who doesn't, right? It's a shock to the system, you soon have to knuckle down or you flunk out. Everything was faster, that is for sure, in and out classrooms.

Talking about fast, everyone has met them, there the guys and girls who talk faster than everyone else and seem smarter than just about everyone else. Smart arse or geeks, there everywhere, from the factory floor to the apartment store and have more mouth than a Bigfoot.

In some ways, you cannot help but listen, everyone crowds round them and you hope that something will rub off on you. That is the theory. Well, I knew one alright, you can call him Tim, that is not his real name, but it does rhyme with dim, he was bright but not all the time.

Tim was a typical geek with glasses to match his image; he had the talk, and could walk the walk. Hey, maybe I am being a bit hard on the lad, but looking back I think he would agree he was a geek who could not shut up, but he was still a likeable lad who was sometimes a laugh. It wasn't always easy for me as nearly everyone was so much younger than me. My own children were about the same age as some of these students I was working with. Making friends with Tim was more by accident you could say than design. I ended up working with Tim and another lad on one of those group projects that are assigned to you by a tutor at college.

Sometimes I think we spent more time looking at the porn the other lad had on his computer rather than doing what we should. Being young they were finding out about the world, and I wasn't going to stop them.

You know sometimes you should listen to your gut feeling (intuition), that is telling you something isn't quite right, instead you go headlong with the talk the talk and the walk the walk and you don't believe he is wrong until you fail. I had my doubts but I wasn't confident enough to challenge Tim. I didn't think we understood the question we were being asked.

We failed miserably, I remembered questioning Tim before we started and finished about whether we were on the right track but being bias I believed what Tim said. I mean he sounded so right and he was so smart, well, at least that is what I thought at the time.

Just because someone's smart doesn't mean there're always right, and that's what I mean by the bias. I let it get in the way of my reasoning.

When we got to see the tutor we didn't get a poor mark as I had expected from him, we got absolute zero. We failed to hit the ball park, we didn't warrant any score, as a team we scored zilch. It taught me a big lesson. It's not always easy to abandon the ship when it isn't sinking.

Tim was embarrassed and it hurt his ego, but hopefully he learnt a valuable lesson too. I don't pretend to know the answer to everything; if I did maybe I would be living in Barbados drinking a Long Island ice tea with not a care in the world. I have made plenty of mistakes, and I try to use them as an opportunity to live a better life with the knowledge I have found. My philosophy is now always, *read between the lines,* determine what the reasoning is behind the author's argument in support of this argument or to criticise its suggestion.

Remember we grow up with what I call *excess baggage*, we can get it from our parents, our schools, and also from our friends and foes, and it takes hard work to negate it from our reasoning to form an honest opinion without bigotry or bias. I have had to work hard to get rid of all the *excess baggage* I grew up with from my parents and my grandmother. I think someone should give me a medal for the shit I have had to deal with and break the cycle.

Remember when you are asked to critically analyse or apply critical thinking in any situation always read through twice what you are being asked to evaluate. When you have done this task make notes of the argument presented and its reasoning and support your evaluation or criticism with relevant evidence in your evaluation. It's all right sometimes to have an opposing view as long as you can back your argument with reasoning and relevant evidence. Don't fall into that trap of letting your bias get in the way of your reasoning and or the evidence.

I can always remember what my grandfather would say to me, *'Don't believe everything you read in the newspapers.'* Every since then, I guess, I have always questioned what I hear on the TV and read in the newspapers. I just needed the confidence to challenge Tim. You have to find out for yourself and believe what you want to believe.

The Greek word for philosophy is *philosophia,* which literally means, the love of wisdom, *(wikipedia 2010).* Sometimes I wish I had more wisdom, but there is the rub it's not until that grey hair starts sprouting from everywhere that you might start to acquire it.

In my philosophy I talk about critical thinking because it's my experience that can help people make that journey of understanding themselves. Sometimes I like to describe much of my life as breaking the cycle. I do n0t mean not repeating mistakes I have made and that is bad enough we all seem to do that. No! Understanding your past for what it is and moving on, that is my philosophy.

In a sense I am standing there right now, observing life, trying to make some sense of the future, ready with my pencil and paper on any street corner, ready to scribble down my wisdom.

So don't get caught in that trap of allowing your assertions or bias to railroad your reasoning. I have had to stop myself many a time from getting on that soapbox, just as much as the *truth never lies,* think before you leap. We all make assumptions; and I try not to make assumptions because invariably I am wrong.

Philosophy can address many different issues, without rational argument as discussed here with critical thinking than even a street philosophy is barking up the wrong tree.

Try to remember it's your bias that leads you astray and your assumptions that clouds your memory. Otherwise, it's a bit like learning a new phone number; it's not long before you've forgotten the old one. Don't take anything I say as gospel, try it and if it works then great. Remember we don't all walk the same path, each of our journeys are different.

In my view critical evaluation can be used in any situation where you need to present an argument. Being able to argue your case is something we don't always have to employ a lawyer for, but there are occasions when we should.

Remember the author may have relied on false evidence or assumptions in forming the argument, so it's up to you to ascertain in your analysis why this is true or not by presenting contrary evidence and reasoning in your critical analysis. Just remember Kiki's and Tim's mistakes. We all make mistakes. I know I do.

Remember we don't all wear the same shoes, skills take time, but we can all learn to have a more balanced view. I have had to get rid of a lot *excess baggage* from my parents and grandmother before I could begin to break the cycle. So before you get on that soapbox think about what you have to say. This

81

street philosophy is born from the mistakes I have made so hopefully you won't make the same mishaps that I did.

A Mirage – Things You Can't See

"Our knowledge is a receding mirage in an expanding desert of ignorance,"
by Will Durant

It was late December 2004, I was 46 years old and basically broke, I had just finished at university, a late starter you could say, but I found myself travelling back down south again. Back to the place where I had spent all my married life even though I was now divorced, alone and more or less homeless, but I had a Master's degree.

So there I was back in North Devon, England, the place where my children were born but they were now grown up, living lives of their own. I couldn't place my burden on them. The only place where I had a home was my grandmother's house, which was now empty. She was in hospital suffering with dementia, and we all knew she wasn't coming back. If I thought I was coming back to North Devon for a relaxing holiday, well, that idea soon faded.

At the time the social services and the hospital were on my back like moles, they wanted my grandmother in a residential home fast, one that could cater for her dementia, so they didn't have to worry. Finally, I found my grandmother a place in a residential home, something I had hoped I would never have to do.

The social services didn't care as long as they weren't footing the bill. Also, the social services wanted me to sell granny's home as soon as possible so I could pay the care home fees, which at the time they were paying. On top of that my daughter Colleen was asking me if she could move into granny's place because her and her boyfriend had gone out and bought a dog. Apparently, the landlord of her apartment didn't like the fact she had bought a dog. She had to get out of there and what could I do but say yes, as long as she didn't mind her dad living with them as I had nowhere else to go and I was broke.

Then, one night I experienced a weird event. Shortly after midnight, settling in bed with a cup of tea, it was then that I had what I would describe as a spiritual enlightenment.

Now, I know many readers will find it hard to believe what I am about to describe as they didn't see it. The truth is, that what I experienced I actually believe, but why it happened? To this day I still don't know. Believe what you want to believe, for me it happened and it lasted for about an hour.

I was talking to God or some higher spirit and then it was like a ball of light suspended in the air. That I was communicating with a shiny bright yellowish light twice the size of a regular soccer ball sounds absolutely mad, but that is what was happening.

Similar experiences have been told by people who believe the same as me, that they've had a spiritual enlightenment. Not all phenomenon's' can be answered by science, we have to have faith as well.

Throughout the whole experience I felt perfectly safe, I wasn't frightened, but I did wonder what was going on. I was asking questions and I was getting answers. And I was told everything would be alright. I was even told how the angel Michael had visited the King of Babylon, and why it was so important.

You're probably thinking is this guy is mad, crackers and must have been smoking 'wacky backy' at the time? Well, I wasn't smoking or mad or even hallucinating, and I will tell you why I know in a moment.

Strangely, Colleen didn't hear me talking in the night, even though the bedroom is right next door to hers. I mean we went to bed about the same time, so I thought she would have heard me talking. She said she hadn't heard a word when I asked her in the morning. That is not that unusual though, as we only hear what we what to hear, and she has a tendency to fall a sleep like a log.

Anyway, I have not finished yet. God, no matter whether you believe me or not, told me everything would be alright and I later wrote down the story of the angel Michael and the King of Babylon, which was amazing. On the table by my bed at the time was my camera, so I took a picture of the shiny light, wanting to check whether what I saw was real or at least that is what I told myself: *The camera wouldn't lie.*

Sure enough the picture came out with the shiny yellowish bright ball of light. My SLR Pentax camera, which I still have worked fine. It wasn't a digital camera; this whole experience happened ways before digital cameras were available, so I had to get the film developed first.

Sometime later, I showed the picture to a friend when I told him about my spiritual experience. At first, my friend was sceptical about my experience, saying it was possible that the camera had developed a fault; it was just a coincidence that I had photographed a shiny bright light. But after seeing the photo, he had a different view.

Now, I know coincidence can happen, but I checked the camera by photographing other items in the bedroom with the same light conditions and the camera worked fine. I believe only a fool would believe it was just purely a coincidence and that my camera had developed a fault right at the moment I photographed this ball of light. Oh, by the way, the camera wasn't aimed anywhere near the light bulb when I took the picture.

What do you think about my experience? – Things happen for all kinds of strange reasons that we don't know the answers. I have told a few people and now I am telling the world, most people are going to be sceptical, that is understandable, in a world where science seeks proof and faith relies on hope and belief. I am not trying to convince you.

It's up to you to choose, to see is to believe would you not agree? Well, no, because as I have already said, magicians and illusionists can trick you into believing, but there was no one performing in my bedroom at the time. We need to have faith in things we haven't seen.

Reading about other people who have had similar spiritual experiences confirms my belief that there are such things out there, we just do not fully understand and are yet to understand.

So I say to you that belief is everything and more, and sometimes we just have to have faith. Don't you think it's strange, that our eyes are deceived so easy, and we sometimes believe in our minds that what we see is real? The saying goes *the camera never lies* but again this isn't true.

The image that is taken by the camera depends on a variety of variables; such as whether the photograph was under or over exposed, the position of the photographer relative to the image, what type of film or lens was used and so on, these all affect and distort the final image, much like a mirage can distort what we actual see.

To see is to believe or is it really just an illusion sometimes - when we lose our sight we have to rely on our other senses to guide us around. Those senses become stronger, more intense, allowing us to function in a world blind to us, allowing us to be fully aware of what's around us. Jesus said, "*Why is it that a blind man believes in me, yet those that can see, do not.*" We can call this blind faith or just faith, even for those with eyes to see and those that haven't seen.

If all it takes are slight air temperature differences to bend the light and form mirages and fool our minds into seeing something that is not there, then what else is there that the eyes can be fooled by. Is it because our minds like to be deceived by an illusion? Or is it because our eyes are not fully developed and they can only perceive to a certain resolution.

It wasn't until the microscope was first invented that we saw another world – a parallel world of microscopic living organisms. A world so small we didn't even know it existed. Yet, it was there all the time, living side by side with us.

Isn't it strange that our limited vision prevented us from viewing this micro environment as if evolution had decided we didn't need to know about its existence? For hundreds of thousands of years this micro world was as alien to us as a man from Mars. But then our minds and our intelligence had decided it was time we understood its existence. I guess, if we could see what was crawling around in our beds at night we would end up becoming insomniacs or zombies.

We have to have faith in things we can't see or haven't experienced. Just as a mirage can fools us and a magician can trick us, our minds are not limited by what we see, but it's only in our beliefs we can overcome this illusion.

Changing My Perspective

"Progress is impossible without change, and those who cannot change their minds cannot change anything,"
by George Bernard Shaw

As the weeks passed I started having some weird experiences, like one night when I was just about to go bed with a cup of tea I suddenly took all my clothes off and went outside. I was walking down the road naked in the middle of the night shouting out loud to everyone I was God. Luckily most people were in bed otherwise they would have got a shock to see me striding down the road claiming to be, God stark naked. I made my way to the town centre and it wasn't long before the police arrived.

My daughter had phoned the police. Good thing she did because who knows what the people in town would have thought of me. The police let me go the following day with no charges, which was unusual.

Anyway, apart from being broke and more or less homeless I was about to suffer one of the biggest setbacks and disappointments of my life. In some ways it was the kind of event that would destroy many people, it nearly did me.

A few weeks passed and there I was lying in a bed of a Mental Health ward having been sectioned under the Mental Health Act. The previous months had been hairy to say the least; I had been having many hallucinations and scaring people with my behaviour.

At the time, I didn't understand why I was in hospital – I didn't realise how ill I was and what danger I posed to myself and others. When my brain had its normal moments all I could think about was the 5 years that I had spent studying for a new career only to come crashing down - my new career had been cut short before it even got started.

I was angry that I had been diagnosed with bipolar disorder. To me it was just a break down caused by stress. Great I thought! I had wasted a lot of time, money and effort only to find myself with a chronic disorder that was likely to make it extremely difficult for me to get that high paid job in the future – the career I had been in search of for many years.

My time in hospital seemed a complete waste of my time – this is what I told the doctors and myself; there was nothing wrong with me apart from being under too much stress. By this time the local health services had put more pressure on me to sell my grandmother's house to pay for care home fees and I was stressed right up to my eye balls. I was ill alright, but I didn't realise it at the time.

Denial was part of the bipolar syndrome though I wasn't aware of this at the time of my hospitalisation. In time I came to accept that I couldn't deal with high levels of stress. Analysing the setback and looking at the positives I decided to write about my time at university as a way of dealing with my disappointment.

While I was undertaking my masters I had told many friends that I wanted to write a book that would help other students. I don't like to say something and then not follow it through, that is me.

It's easy to look at setbacks with anger that things haven't quite turned out the way you had expected. Yet, the more I look at setbacks now the more I believe in a different perspective so that when we encounter them we can use them to our advantage. I took the disappointment of possibly not being able to do a high powered IT job in the future because of the stress level as a blessing. Whatever the future held for me it had to be less stressful. I knew I had to view this setback as an advantage as much as possible because I couldn't change what had happened to me.

Changing your perspective and the way you view setbacks will make it easier to overcome the problems you encounter. Sounds so Simple Simon doesn't it? Hey, simple things are often the best.

Now, when I relax I try to analyse setbacks by looking at the positives, then the setbacks look less significant. When you have less anger you can see more clearly. I try to look at the positive aspects as much as possible.

Let's not belittle setbacks as trivial, by having a positive outlook we can try and overcome them to our advantage. Remember these wise words, *"the only thing that stands between a man and what he wants from life is often merely the will to try it and the faith to believe that it is possible,"* by Richard M. DeVos the co-founder of Amway a multi-national business. With positive actions and thoughts we can accomplish so much more than with just wise words.

By training our minds to focus on the advantages, however they might present themselves, we can view any obstacle in a different light. We call this positive thinking. The more control we have over our mind in a positive manner, the easier it will be to limit the destructive force it could have on us. This way of thinking would later show me that bipolar could actually have some advantages for me.

Our brain is a powerful organism, which even today; with all the advancements in technology, we still today, nowhere near fully understand the workings of the brain. Apparently, we only use about ten percent of what we could be using of our brains capacity. The ability to understand and control our mind and use it for positive pursuits is a skill we should all learn to utilize. If we can exploit our minds in a positive way it's easier to obtain want we want.

It's like the genie in the bottle – popularized in the book *1001 Tales of the Arabian Nights*, we ask and we shall receive. After a good rub, the genie comes from within the magic lamp and we should wish for what it will grant us. We can use this story in a literal sense, as if we are the genie, able to think about our wish so they become true.

Understanding bipolar is about teaching your mind to believe that you can actually get better. So by teaching your mind that bipolar can be a positive thing, you can begin to look at its advantages with open eyes, which can have many therapeutic benefits and stop you dwelling on the negatives. Try this strategy to help combat setbacks. None of this advice is easy when you suffer a major disappointment as I did, but what else was there to do except continue walking naked down the street.

The Truth Never Lies

"Three things cannot be long hidden: the sun, the moon, and the truth,"
by Buddha

It had been several weeks now since my forced incarceration under auspices of the Mental Health Act under a section 28. It was 2005 when my world came crashing down around me. My hallucinations and weird behaviour were symptomatic of the diagnosis for bipolar disorder.

Finally, I had been correctly diagnosed after all the years of suffering with manic depression. I was in hospital recovering from a manic episode, which then finally showed the doctors the problems which had so dogged my life. Although I was angry at times with being diagnosed bipolar, I slowly came to terms with my situation.

Nearing the end of my stay in hospital I made friends with another patient, a nice, softly spoken and caring woman, yet who was also on a ward for the mentally ill. Although I had seen Susan many times on the ward I was mostly in a world of my own. I was transfixed and often felt as though I was being persecuted by persons unknown. The paranoia surrounded me like a pack of wild dogs. I was suspicious of everything and everyone. Before the forced stay in hospital I was convinced people were out to kill me.

My permanent suspicious attitude showed while meeting new people and in nearly everything I did. At the time, I was living with my daughter and sleeping in the spare bedroom. It was my daughter and her boyfriend that had to call the police to protect me from myself one time, something which at the time I didn't appreciate.

Believing that some friends of my daughter were IRA members, I had gone completely bonkers. While in hospital I even believed that the people I had met at my daughter's home were now appearing in the grounds of the hospital, which just reinforced my beliefs in the IRA syndrome. I believed they were checking up on me.

I was ill alright, but subconsciously I just didn't want to believe it. During my stay in hospital I was seeing all sorts and even thought I was James Bond. Unsupervised at one stage I was driving around as if I was the 007 action hero, even though I didn't have the DB7, it was crazy.

I don't think the doctors realised I was driving around in my car while I was unsupervised otherwise I doubt they would have allowed me out. The medications clearly stated, do not drive, but I had no control and I certainly wasn't aware of my actions and how disastrous it could have been for me, and the general public.

Susan would talk to me about the Bible and how it had helped her through her break down. Gradually, she would tell me about what had happened to her during that time. Even when I was ill, I could still feel emotion although I must have appeared as though detached from reality. At times all I could think about was me and what had happened.

My family appeared at first to abandon me, making me feel sure I'd been miss-diagnosed and that I was merely suffering with too much stress. They didn't understand what bipolar meant, and nor did I at the time. It took several more years before I would finally understand and come to terms with the diagnosis.

Susan explained that apparently her husband had left her for another woman, and with middle age catching up with her she couldn't cope anymore and had a total mental break down. I felt sorry for her because I also felt as though everyone around me had abandoned me. Then one Sunday, during the few hours we were unsupervised, Susan invited me to her local church service because she said, *'I would enjoy the atmosphere.'* Susan would often quote from the Bible, which appeared to comfort her while she recovered in hospital.

Everyone gathered in the large sports hall of the local college and sang jubilant songs. It was packed, more like a rock concert than any church I'd been to before. I didn't mind the atmosphere, it was electric with joy. Suddenly the crowd were silent as the preacher rose to the pulpit to begin his sermon of the gospel; you couldn't hear a pin drop, just the occasional chorus of agreement from the crowd as the preacher spoke. While listening to the preacher reading from the Bible and talking about Jesus, it came to me, almost like a divine message.

Yet in the quietness of the room, the message I received told me to say just three simple words, 'truth never lies.' Everyone looked around at me, even the preacher, his eyes leaving the bible – nothing was said, but I believe everyone would agree that it was a bolt out of the blue, like it was meant to be.

The message that the *truth never lies* has stayed with me in my consciousness ever since that day. There was no hesitation in my prose, nor any time for reflection. I had no control. It was a message to everyone and it sure was a message that I had never had before or since.

Looking around as I spoke the words, I could see the preacher's reddened face and clearly see an expression of agreement. I didn't feel embarrassed, I felt good inside, as the words had come from God. And so it was that I would choose those simple three words for the title of this book, which I knew I must write.

It's Never Too Late

A Different Kind of Love

"Love is the beauty of the soul,"
by Saint Augustine

After, I came out of hospital feeling dejected and almost worthless. The medication was taking its toll, sometimes I felt like a zombie. My mouth would froth with spit and sometimes I could not stop talking. Friends and family would often have to tell me to shut up; otherwise I had just rattled on relentlessly. Sometimes I would exaggerate or even lie, but that was the bipolar, it made a mess of me.

Often I would be in another fantasy world without any control, rapid cycling as the doctors called it. It was 2005 and at the time everything seemed to look so fruitless to me. The bipolar was still severe, with the illness wrecking how I felt about everything around me. Still, I was yet to realise how ill I actually was. It's only now looking back that I realise how my family and friends must have felt seeing me that way, unable to help.

At the time I was living with a friend who offered to take me on holiday to India, to help him record and photograph the plight of the elusive Bengal tiger. At first I was a bit apprehensive about going to India. From the stories he'd told me about previous trips to India the jungle sounded pretty scary. Reluctantly, I agreed to help him on his charity photographic assignment.

Though I'd seen many TV shows about India I was still very excited to see it for myself, even if I did still have doubts about the jungle. Forget about what you've seen on TV because it doesn't prepare you at all for the shock of departing from the comfort of the air-conditioned plane. Leaving the airport the hot air grasps at your throat, you can almost taste an Indian curry in the wind. We sped our way to the hotel in a taxi surrounded by a haze of dust, a whole multitude passed by. Both young and old were driving their carts and cattle beside the speeding rickshaws, the dusty Mercedes, Fords and Toyotas didn't seem to matter. People begging by the side of the road, street vendors selling their hot food, a huge diversity of life, rich and poor, everywhere jam packed, the sound of many horns, everyone impatient as if there's no time to waste.

Every traffic light we stopped at we got pestered by people of all ages wanting to sell us their goods or just begging for any spare change. I saw the contrast of a woman with a small child looking like they hadn't washed in months with rags for clothes. Compared to the homeless back in England these people were a lot worse off. I couldn't help but give money to the woman and child; it just seemed the right thing to do.

We had arrived in New Delhi, the capital city of the northern tip of India. We had decided to stay here for a couple of nights before flying to Jabalpur where we would hire a vehicle to travel the 200 kms or so to Kanha National Park. I had decided to research the Kanha National Park, a Tiger Reserve situated in *Madhya Pradesh* the central province of India, by reading a scientific account of the wildlife that had been written some year's earlier by a leading expert. I wanted to understand the issues that faced not only the Bengal tiger, but also the many other animals whose existence is threatened. I thought that I wouldn't like the jungle partly because of the bugs and the fear of being eaten by a tiger.

My fears were heightened by the bipolar making me imagine all sorts of scenarios. Contrary to these fears I really enjoyed everyday even though it was an early start. As a child I never liked to see animals caged up in zoos, so the jungle was an adventure and a chance see nature as it was intended. Everyday was like therapy for me, in my view it doesn't get much better than having fresh air and some sort of routine.

Our first day in the park was an early start up at 4.00 am, and into the jeep by 4.30, it's more like a jungle than a park, and there's no fence surrounding its boundary. We would spend the day searching for the elusive tigers with the Indian Mahouts (elephant handlers), who ride and steer the elephants through the jungle.

We were safely tucked away in to the wooden cradle that they call the *howdah*, which is strapped onto the back of the elephant. The natural instinct for an elephant is to run away for miles if they come close to a tiger, but because of their training and the wooden stick the Mahouts use on the elephants they are cajoled into getting close to the tigers. To me it seems cruel, you could sometimes hear the elephant snorting and panting loudly while we were only a few feet away from a resting tiger, the Mahout's stick was a constant reminder to the elephant.

The jungle was alive with the sounds of langur monkeys, who alert the other animals of any approaching tigers. The monkeys would know from a considerable distance if a tiger was in the vicinity. Other animals including bison and deer would hear the call of the monkey and the heightened tension would spark a frenzied movement from the grazing animals.

Over the days and weeks we spent tracking the tigers by their *pugmarks* (paw prints) I got used to being cradled by these majestic animals; the elephant was our friend and companion. We saw how the elephants were fed and we watched how they played while washing in the river. They are beautiful animals and we should do everything we can to save every last one. Although there are no wild elephants in Kanha, there are some in other parts of India, and it would seem that they are just as threatened as the Bengal tiger.

Before leaving for India I wanted to gain a different perspective of India, so I acquired *Travels on my Elephant*, by Mark Shand. I'm glad I brought the book with me to while away the nights, reading in my room at the royal lodge where we stayed.

There wasn't much else to do, well the food was good, so we did plenty of eating, but we seemed to have a different flavoured Indian curry dish at every meal. The book is about Mark's love affair with a female elephant called Tara, which he bought at an Indian elephant market and rode 1600 kms across India on her back. It's a documentary about being a part of rural life across India, and also the love that Mark felt for Tara.

I got to know Tara and became more comfortable about being with the elephants that I rode on my daily trips into the jungle. I won't tell you what happened to Tara because I think it's up to you to find out. All I can say is that love is a many flavoured spring, it can appear and sprout from anywhere, just as it did for me each day showing me beautiful glimpses into the lives of these animals in their natural jungle habitat.

This was a different kind of love. A love that I know many readers will have experienced, and which helped me come to terms with my illness. I found thinking about the plight of animals a relief from the distress of dealing with bipolar disorder.

When we talk about love, sometimes the love that we can have for animals can be just as rewarding if not more so than our partners in life. The more we appreciate that love is a gift that we can share and give, the better the world will be. I certainly found that love for animals helped me to cope with the bipolar and the black cloud of depression that had surrounded me before I left for India. My pleasure in life had been reawakened by a new love for animals.

The Black Cloud that Surrounds Me

"He, who has health, has hope. And he who has hope, has everything,"
an Arabian Proverb

The times when I am in manic depression mode I later like to refer to as living under a black cloud. I believe many of you may be able to identify with this analogy. *'There's always tomorrow,'* that is what I say to myself when I am in my darkest hours.

Try to remember this phrase because I believe it will help you overcome those moments when life doesn't seem worth living, it's a strategy I use all the time. A similar strategy is what I use to cope with bipolar, but you can also use this to cope with similar moments of depression when that black cloud arrives. It does make a difference, when the dark demons surround me like smoke from a burning fire.

Sometimes you don't understand why you are depressed, it just happens and descends upon you without notice. The only real remedy is plenty of rest, exercise and strategies to help combat those demons.

But, who gives a shit, right? Well I do, and I think that those who've chosen to read this book, are bipolar or who have friends and family with the disorder might also agree. It rears its ugly head when you least expect it, and it's difficult to avoid. Many will say not to worry about it but it's been my shadow for so long now, I only wish that blue skies would arrive.

People have no empathy, they don't understand or listen, and they don't know what it's like to live with this black cloud, feeling marginalised in society. It's no wonder I avoid people like the plague sometimes.

I take the medicine, get the headaches, what's the point I ask myself. I see doctors, psychiatrists, counsellors and others, and I try and make them listen. I write letters but I might as well talk to myself – yet I do that anyway. The battle has begun again with me, this endless war. I have no defence, it comes and goes, and I try and fight the demons. I live alone and loneliness is like a tear with no home and sometimes I cry, but no one is there to see my pain. The black cloud affects me in many ways, as I will explain.

Not many years ago now; just after gaining my Master's degree, I can remember being offered a top job with an IT company in London. I had made the six hour journey to London twice for the interviews, everything seemed fine. I had the confidence to go to the interviews and answer all the questions, yet in the end my self-confidence vanished, leaving me a wreck.

Confidence, I did have it but in the end it let me down, and disappeared like the wind as if it was never there. Worrying about how I would cope in a new job, at the last minute I turned the job offer down. Family and friends thought I was mad to do that, but they didn't understand, they couldn't see inside me. My confidence was a mess, and I now know that I was still very ill inside, something you can't see but its still there. I hadn't long come out of hospital but the bipolar was still quite manic.

I could easily hide my illness and even today I do sometimes hide it. Yes, I have two arms, two legs, but inside I am missing so much that you can't see, and I know unless you have experienced it you will not understand. That black cloud had cast its shadow and with all the emotion I was feeling – the rejection, the feeling of being alone, I think it's a miracle I didn't commit suicide.

In fact I was almost there; it was only the phone call from my daughter that saved me. There had been plenty of occasions when I have been so close to leaving this world behind. So you see, the black cloud is invisible to you, but it's always ready to descend upon me.

It's strange looking back now, but at the time I didn't realise that this new career which had so consumed much of my time before, really wasn't for me. I didn't understand this until a couple years later, when I finally realised a career in computing wasn't actually what I wanted. The initial setback was difficult to accept. I didn't yet see the setback as an opportunity, until I began to question who I was and what was right for me. I now look back at those times in hospital with sadness at how ill I was and at the fact that even though those around me could see how ill I was, I could not.

When I felt abandoned and alone and was contemplating suicide I didn't realise how vulnerable I was and was totally unaware of my situation. It's perhaps because I am a strong character that I was able to pull through, even without the support of family or friends at the time.

Though I can write that I don't want your sympathy or your empathy, which it is I do not know or care. I take the medicine, but I also suffer with the headaches, and the loneliness is this black cloud that hovers over me like a hangman's noose. This illness cannot be seen, but it still hides within me, and I fight with it everyday and I try. I try so hard to force myself to meet people but I find this difficult and sometimes threatening. So I end up backing away and retreating to the safety of my home. I find it difficult to trust people, even though I am lonely. I have tried to get support but it makes me feel marginalised and alone in this modernity.

Sometimes, doctors or psychiatrists try to categorise you as if one remedy will fit just because it works on others. They talk about how celebrities cope which makes me think, *"Well, we don't all wear the same shoes."* It is common for the experts to try and fit you into a labeled shoebox along with others that appear similar.

Take my doctor; he or she is more like a career's counsellor, always blabbing on about how Steven Fry and other celebrities cope with bipolar, yet are still able to work. I wish he or she would just shut the fuck up because their arguments do not stack up, otherwise mine's a size eight.

Again, if I wanted to work I would get a job, and when I feel ready. The last thing you want is to force someone back to work because of political correctness that isn't ready, and then they turn into homicidal maniacs.

Just because of political correctness or the latest fad dreamed up by some lemon head in a government department, they attack the people with mental issues as likely candidates for a return to work.

Now let's get this straight, to all you lemon heads out there I have got a serious mental disorder recognised as a disability under law. Why do you think I have regular counselling? Why do you think I take anti-psychotic drugs? Is it starting to sink in, do you get the picture yet or maybe you haven't got enough brain cells to take it in.

I feel that I am on a mission that is why I wrote this book, to tell the world and give people the chance to listen to my story. If you knew every detail, which you do not because I have concealed so much to protect myself, then maybe you would have a different view. If I told you every detail it would shock you and you'd probably switch off like most people do, they don't want to hear the truth because the truth hurts. Well how do you think I feel inside? I have lived through it and have had to deal with it all. I keep it inside, trapped like a prisoner in a cell, locked away and forgotten about.

I think that I am lucky in some ways like that I am still here and that I have had the strength to survive. The wounds I have got are on the inside not the outside, most of you have no idea what it's like, and I have been the victim.

Sometimes I will have order and then other times complete disorder, which is a common routine for me, and my moods will change, up and down. Rapid cycling they call it, one minute high as a kite, the next a deep black depression where nothing matters and you can't do anything about it.

I often feel guilty, not because I've done anything wrong; it's just that I feel that society looks at mental illness in a simplistic way. The average Joe on the street might say to someone with deep depression, just take some aspirins and get on with it.

Even the medical profession and governments look at mental illness with a low priority; although bipolar is recognised as a disability it's often misunderstood in society. People hear about their friends or family members who perhaps are suffering with depression and they see it as something that you can just shrug off.

Until recently governments took a low key approach to mental illness, choosing to lock people up in institutions rather than seek research into the causes of mental illness.

As you read my stories you might have a better understanding of those of us that have been diagnosed with bipolar disorder. Living with a black cloud hanging over me is the only way I can explain the way I feel about this disorder.

This book is not a medical remedy for bipolar, but a collection of stories that reflect my experience and viewpoint that I hope will sometimes make you laugh and possibly help you reflect on your life. I swing on a tree between two extremes; black and white or Jekyll and Hyde. But life's a bitch, right! But living with bi-polar disorder is even more of a roller coaster ride. As you will see...

It's Never Too Late

Predict the Future

"The future belongs to those who believe in the beauty of their dreams,"
by Eleanor Roosevelt.

Listen to your heart beating, each breath gives you life but we are *dead men walking* the moment it stops and your future is no more.

Sometimes you think you can see the future but if you could would you alter it? We have as humans the capacity to sometimes predict the future, but we fail to use it when it happens. A blind man doesn't see anything, a man with eyes may see many things and a wise man will see beyond the peripheral.

Many of us avoid our intuitions, yet they often remind us in subtle ways to avoid certain scenarios. They say that we can have a bad feeling about something before it has happened; again it is our intuition that lets us know if something isn't quite right.

The distinction between prediction and intuition is the difference between knowing something is going to happen and just having the feeling that something is about happen.

After being diagnosed bipolar I became deeply worried about my future; what I mean by this is I had a lot of problems and a lot to worry about in the future, if I had a future at all. I would spend many days and hours with the problems troubling my mind. Problems would follow me like my shadow. It wasn't my bipolar, even though that was troubling enough, it was something I can't discuss and it consumed my every thought.

Then one day I was at a business seminar at a local hotel and it was there I met a woman that eventually eased my sickness. Looking back, I think that I meet people, who are to me messengers or angels that guide my path when I need them, when my heart is open and ready to receive them.

Anyway, it was strange our meeting. I didn't know the woman but she seemed to know me; what I mean by this is, she said something to me that only I could know.

Amazed and intrigued, I wanted to know more about her. She told me she was a shaman and had predicted many events and done readings for celebrities such as the former Prime Minister John Major. Her name was Leticia Parmer, astrologer to the stars. Immediately I made an appointment to see her and to have my reading done. It was there at her home that I learnt much about myself and about shamanism.

Several visits later at her home, one having been to have my reading done and two more that were to heal my body which was ill from the stress of the problem that I had been constantly worried about.

After these meetings with Leticia I felt much better, we had worked out my reading and what I needed to do that was, at the moment, holding me back in my life. Healing my body by a shaman performing the ritual of burning *salvia-divinorum* while dancing and chanting around my body which felt good, it seemed to lift away the evil spirits that had entered my body.

The problem that had followed me as if it were my shadow, which I explained fully to Leticia, was something I was desperate to know the outcome of. Leticia told me what would happen. She said, *"Don't worry it will be ok, but it won't end like you are expecting it to though."*

And sure enough several months later the problem that had been my shadow was over and it didn't end like I was expecting it to either, as Leticia had predicted. Leticia spent a lot of time helping me and I thank her now, as I did then.

Sometimes we have dreams that foretell of things that indeed could be fortunate for those of us that can learn how to interpret them. I can tell you of many times that I have had dreams where I have been given numbers but not then followed those numbers in say the lottery.

I have learned that dreams come to help us, but it's up to us to learn how to understand their meaning. Numbers are great for accounting but not a lot of good if you are starving and all you have is a bean counter. Seriously, I believe that we all have the ability to see the future and make predictions; yet, we haven't developed that capability sufficiently to fully utilise this gift.

There have been many people that claim to have seen the future, for instance Nostradamus in his book *The Prophecies* and other soothsayers.

But what about prediction, do we really have the ability to see into the future? Do our dreams open a door to another world where we can see the future? Is it possible that when we dream our future is trying to communicate with us? We just can't always understand the messages that come to us.

Maybe, when we dream other dreamers are trying to communicate with us, a bit like a radio transmission where sometimes it's fuzzy and unclear but other times we can clearly interpret the message. Maybe the messages we get are like ciphers, encrypted so that only we can de-cipher them, because we hold the keys to understanding them.

Like why is it that I never get to sit next to a beautiful blond? You travel and fly to different places but the airlines companies never seem to place me next to a stunning woman. I usually end up sitting with an overweight grouch. Only joking, but I can predict that scenario quite accurately.

I believe that in our dreams sometimes we are in direct communication with people whom we love and they want to warn us of things we should avoid. I was told that in some cultures they believe that who ever is helping us through our dreams can't directly communicate the exact numbers or information with us, some believe this to be God's work. Some cultures believe that for instance maybe the numbers communicated should actually be reversed to be correct.

We could say that prediction may be a power we haven't explored enough, whereas some of us appear to have mastered the art quite successfully. It would seem that our dreams could be a message vehicle, of which we don't fully understand its mechanics. Our dreams are perhaps the gateway to the future...

The Butterfly and the Bee

"If music be the food of love, play on,"
by William Shakespeare

As the years passed since being diagnosed with bipolar I slowly started to break out of my shell. It was the summer of 2007 and I was living along the coast not far from Brighton, England at a place called Peacehaven.

Aptly named as such at the end of the imaginary Meridian Line, was a town where I could come to terms with my bipolar and start a new life. I could walk along the chalk cliffs or go down to the beach and sit and watch the waves break on the pebbles. I got out more through exploring nearby towns just for a gentle walk and a beer. Regularly I would go to salsa dancing, sometimes more than once a week. It seemed I was coming out of my shell again, ready to face the world.

I would use the internet to find out about interesting local places to visit. Ever since a young boy I'd always liked history like where I would read many books about the Romans and the ancient world.

Another fascination was exploring English castles, I remember the time when my grandmother took me to see Carmarthen castle in Wales. There were also the ruins at Tintagel in Cornwall in which I explored that first time I came to the West Country, all those years ago.

During my internet search I came across the Long Man of Sussex which was a short car journey from Peacehaven, near a village called Wilmington. I just had to see this for myself. As I drove out into the countryside it was a beautiful hot summer's day, it was a glorious feeling to be alive.

Driving along I passed by an ancient forest called the Seven Sisters and I could see the rolling hills of the Sussex downs and a large horse carved into the side of a hill in the distance.

As I snaked onwards I passed a small village with a sign that said, *'Beware of frogs crossing.'* I could feel the goodness of being with nature and the countryside. I found myself thinking: *It would be nice to live here, a small village away from the noise of suburban life.*

As I approached the village of Wilmington I could just see out of the corner of my right eye, the giant chalk carving of the Long Man of Sussex. I stopped the car and got out to view the huge image set against the steep hill. In the distance I could just make out some people, who were making there way to the foot of the hill, they looked like ants compared to the size of the chalk figure.

The Long Man is a chalk carving over 200 feet long on one of the hills that surrounds the village of Wilmington.

Nobody knows when this image was carved into the side of the hill to reveal the natural chalk, or who carved it or why? There are many interesting mysteries surrounding the Long Man and just as many old tales about its purpose, one such is that it was used as a phallic symbol to encourage procreation among the villagers. Horny or not, it was made for reasons unknown.

I decided I would make my way towards the Long Man and walk along the path I had seen other people earlier endeavouring to get close to the figure. As I walked along the path across some fields the figure became even larger you could see the scale of this carving as you got ever closer. I decided I would head for a smaller hill beneath the Long Man and rest for awhile. As I sat there viewing in the distance the Sussex downs I felt at ease with myself and the world and decided I would compose a poem.

It was a beautiful day you couldn't help but feel good about life. Able to appreciate the beauty of nature the summer sun and a gentle cool breeze I relaxed and lay there thinking: *I'd been lucky to have made it this far in life.*

As I made my way back to the car along the path I decided I would explore the village. Walking down into the village amongst the hedgerows and deciduous trees some overgrown and offering shade to the heat of the sun I passed an old abbey some of which had fallen into disrepair. As walked on to my left I saw an iron gate leading to the church where much was overgrown with bramble along its path.

As I entered the church grounds I could see a majestic old yew tree amongst the grave stones, it was massive, with many branches being supported by sturdy wooded props. I would find out later that the yew tree was over 1600 years old and still going strong.

The old yew was a welcome shade from the summer sun as I gazed at the entrance to the church. Set in amongst the Sussex downs of rolling countryside and gentle hills the church was small and quaint, built from stone that had weathered countless storms. Apparently, some parts of the church were found to date back to the 12th century so I found out later.

Looking at the entrance to the church I saw a darkened oak Norman shape door, which had a beauty of its own; the door had an age to the wood, you wondered what tales it could tell. Approaching the door which was beneath an open porch, I wasn't sure it would be unlocked as I tried repeatedly to open the door. Just as I was about to give up, the door opened if by magic like a command *open sesame.*

Thinking: *Someone had opened the door from the inside.* I was shocked to see no one as I entered and looked around, the church was empty only one living soul and that was me.

Strangely, I felt like someone wanted me to come in. Looking around the church I wasn't spooked by the experience but it did open my spiritual mind. It was then that I saw the butterfly and the bee. A beautiful stained glass window with the words of Jesus from the gospel of Thomas, *Raise the stone, and thou will find me; cleave the wood, and there I am.*

Many times I have been back to the church which caught my imagination and gave me a feeling that everything would be alright. Somehow it was mystical and spiritual at the same time. Severely months later, even in my darkest moments I had the inspiration to paint a picture of the butterfly and bee stained glass window. And did I pray? Yes I did!

The butterfly and the bee was my quest to see its beauty for myself.

Living with Bipolar

"It's easier to go down a hill than up it but the view's much better from the top,"
by Arnold Bennett

It was 2008 and I was trying to cope with bipolar and at the same time deal with my aging grandmother. I was aware she could die at anytime she had reached the grand age of 95 and deteriorating fast with dementia.

Although, granny had at times been spiteful to me throughout my life, I had cared for her to many years not feel compassion towards her. And, I would remember what the Buddhist's say about respecting your elders because without them you would not be here.

The Buddhist's believers feel a social and moral obligation to look after their parents and elderly members of their families, no matter how difficult and costly that might be. I felt the same even though my grandmother at times had made me feel I want to hate her. She was all I knew for much of my life, I just had to respect that even though deep inside my heart she had caused me so much pain. Like the time when she refused to accept Karen my future wife because she lived on a council estate, the wrong neighbourhood. All I wanted was for my grandmother to respect Karen instead she ignored her all her life.

My grandmother also ignored her grandchildren most of the time favouring Colleen sometimes over my son Jamie, which I didn't like. She had a mixed up way of showing love if it was love, something that I believe she couldn't do.

There was much about my father I didn't like also, I guess he inherited it from my grandmother like two peas in a pod they were both alike, which I tried to change but failed it was only me that could break the cycle. But I was aware that we are often so concerned with our own life that we fail to look after the very people who brought us into this world. I was always aware that it would be me that could only break the cycle and although they had caused me so much heartache there wasn't much I could do but accept the *status quo*.

Every time I went visiting my grandmother in a home for the elderly I often heard about other residents whose families failed to come and visit them. I felt so sad for them, left alone in care homes.

Believe me it wasn't easy to take the responsibility for my grandmother but the task had fallen at my door, there was nobody else to take the responsibility - at times I wasn't in good health myself coping with bipolar. I just had no choice my father had died many years earlier, and even if he hadn't somehow I don't think he would have cared for granny, he hated her too much.

I had a lot of hate for my grandmother as well, but over the years I had turned a lot of that hate to sympathy. I guess I had grown up with too much love in me to hate everything and everyone. God had given me more love than to hate.

As I would sit there looking at my grandmother and the last thing I needed was to see my own mortality, face to face, my grandmother aging like a decaying vegetable, and me more depressed from the experience. But, it taught me a lot, you have to face death as a process of living you can't ignore the evitable.

As much as I wanted to forget my responsibility I could not, I sat there hand in hand with my grandmother in a room full of patients with similar conditions trying to overcome my fear. And, it was a fear, a fear that maybe this would be my fate someday, to be left with just maybe your memories if you were lucky. Even though I was uncomfortable with the experience I knew I was doing the right thing. Over the years I'd cared for granny something inside me grew, a deeper understanding of what it is to love without gain.

I could n0t help thinking that maybe granny had been neglected and not loved as a child and although it hadn't been easy for me I just had the strength to break the cycle so that my children could grown up with the love I know they have.

Now, I try to teach my children the skills and experience that I have learnt in case they someday may need them. But it's a different generation; they seem to have a perspective of life surrounded by gizmos and gadgets. The number of times I see teenagers constantly peering into their mobile phones; never looking up, oblivious to the world around them.

Is it any wonder there is a social and parental disconnecting within families? Our children spend more time with computers and less time talking and socialising with each other. It's no wonder there are social problems of serious drug and alcohol abuse among many of our teenagers who often lack the necessary skills of interactions with their peers. Maybe it's just me getting older and prone to moan a lot more.

In many ways I think the disappointment and setback of being diagnosed with bipolar had been another test. Initially there was anger when I was first diagnosed with bipolar but I soon came to accept it and turn it to my advantage. You see you can't go around with hate in your heart for long before it will destroy you and everything around you. Many people and events had hurt me in the past but I could not let that destroy me.

Rising to the challenge and gladden that I hadn't shrugged off my responsibilities knowing I had done my best for my grandmother. Making sure she was adequately cared for I conquered the fear of my mortality. And, this is something I can say I am proud of, that through all the torment of depression I still had the strength to care for my grandmother.

There were many days when the black clouds would descend upon me without warning I just had to live through until another day would come. I always remembered, '*There's always tomorrow.*'

My grandmother had progressive dementia, which is all too common today it would seem in an increasingly aging population. After many years of visiting her in the home she soon began to forget who I was, her memory had vanished like melting snow with brief glimpses of awareness.

I just hope that somewhere along the road she remembered me and that I was there for her in her memories as she passed away on that final journey. I had got to know my elders and although my grandmother had gone I had done my best for her. Even in my darkest moments of bipolar I had coped, and I was proud of that.

Live the Dream

> *"Who looks outside, dreams; who looks inside, awakes,"*
> by Carl Jung

It was early 2010 and spring hadn't arrived and I was still living of a shoestring dreaming of being a writer. Living in a fantasy, in another world, is I guess a preoccupation for many people, we all like to dream. Daydreaming is a habit we can all admit to if we are honest.

There is nothing wrong in fantasying about dating that beautiful blond or winning the lottery. Ever since I can remember I have thought deep about life, and maybe having bipolar a chemical imbalance, has made me challenge the *status quo.*

They say that governments invented the lottery as opium for the masses, as a way of satisfying the dreams of the population. In some ways, the lottery probably does, it allows revenue to be collected for charitable causes, and also satisfies the needs and hopes for many punters. But, I have to admit I have more chance of dating that beautiful blond than winning the lottery.

Let me begin by telling you a tale to this day I still don't know if it was real or just a dream. Some things don't seem real; remember 9/11 and the twin towers crashing down to dust, it was real enough, a terrible tragedy, yet every time you see the film coverage you can't believe your eyes.

According to my shrink I suffer from hallucinations which appear real as any event. In a dream you wake up, realise it was just a dream. Hallucinations are weird; it's as real as it gets, bread and butter reality. It appears I have had many; some you can explain some you cannot, yet both seem real. I will let you decide on this one.

Remember, one thing though I hadn't been smoking any wacky backy or drinking alcohol just my daily dose of prescribed medication.

It was classic moonlight night; I had gone to bed and forgotten I had not locked the front door to my apartment, which was typical. Often the front door was unlocked. Besides, I lived on the top floor of an apartment block and you needed a key to open the main entrance to the building.

Thinking: *If someone's going to get in they'll get in.* Besides, the bed was too comfortable and I was too lazy to get out and lock the door. Lazy bastard, I here you say, and you are right, give the guy or gal a medal. Normally, the neighbours are moderately quiet but suddenly all let loose, doors were banging and shutting, my apartment was shaking it felt like an earthquake. I couldn't hear anyone shouting; just the continuing loud banging sound of doors opening and closing, combined with the steps of someone moving beneath or across from my apartment.

Its human nature to listen into a conversation, to be inquisitive, but all I could hear was the loud banging, and the thud of foot steps.

Suddenly, my front door flung open. Boy, oh, boy, did it give me a shock as I heard the door crash against my bedroom wall. Quickly, I sat up ready to leap from my bed, when I saw a naked blond streak pass my bedroom door. Wow! She was mid-thirties I figured; curvaceous, with long blond hair flowing down to generous hips, and I wasn't frightened, just perfectly aroused. I could see her walk straight into my lounge from my bed as she waved her arms and screamed.

Without hesitation I called out and said, "*Its ok.......it's alright,*" but I should have said, "*Stay awhile...........Stay awhile,*" as she immediately turned around and walked straight pass my bedroom out the front door.

The shrinks would say this was a hallucination, but to me it was as real as it gets, bread and butter reality.

Wishing only the blond stayed the night; I could have done with the indulgence of a woman.

Possibly, a neighbour sleep walking I mused, anyhow sometime later I asked the blond in the opposite apartment. Hey, she fitted the description, but she politely said no.

To this day I don't know what happened but it was certainly real enough for me. Dream or hallucination you tell me?

Getting out and walking would sometimes helps me, but I would tend to end up making a routine out of it, then I just completely stop, there's were no half measures, no even balance. Extremes at each end of the scale that's bipolar either I would over do it, or not do it at all, always the excluded middle. Counteracting these imbalances I've tried to put strategies in place to help me, but its not easy being a kind of Jekyll and Hyde person in terms of extremes.

Dreams or no dreams bipolar has become a fashionable label, because of the celebrity status it has been given in the media, with so many celebrities publicly telling the world about there condition. The general public are now more aware of bipolar as a common term than of its manifestations. But, I do worry about the future especially for my children as I hope they don't get bipolar, and have to endure what I've been through.

Hallucinations are a common problem, especially, if you're self medicating, which is something I try to avoid. Thankfully, I realise that illegal drugs or excess alcohol never help, subscribing only to appropriate medication these days.

Plenty of time to relax is important to take away the stress, otherwise, like an elastic band, you stretch it out; it will either snap or go back to normal. If you end up dreaming then so be it, better than spending more time eating, and glued to the telly, please let me dream.

If you don't follow with your dreams you might as well be a canned vegetable. Yes, some people live the dream. But let me tell you a story why you should live the dream, and forget about everything that is stopping you.

Have you ever heard about the incredible story about The *Diving Bell and the Butterfly?* It's a true story written by Jean-Dominique Bauby; it captured my imagination, and made me think long and hard about what I was doing with my life. I first heard about the story really by chance, I was flicking through the TV channels one night, and I came across this documentary film which recalls the life of Jean-Dominique Bauby who was once the editor of the fashionable French magazine Elle.

At first, I didn't know if I would like to watch a film about someone who was so severely disabled. Honestly, we all have the urge sometimes not to look at things we don't want to think about, we would rather think about something else instead. We all do it, look the other way afraid maybe that somehow this might happen to us. Well, I persevered and enjoyed the love of life the film gave me, even though Jean-Dominique Bauby was the soul that life had dealt such a cruel twist.

The film was a portrait memoir of the book *The Diving Bell and the Butterfly* which was written solely by Jean-Dominique Bauby blinking his left eye lid. Suffering at the age of 43 a massive stroke Bauby was left paralysed and speechless apart from the ability to use his left eye for communication.

By using ESA, a technique that uses the frequency of letters of the French language Bauby was able to dictate words, sentences, and eventually the book with the aid of his editor. Every word counts in this book, you know that Bauby's effort was enormous, never lingering always with purpose.

That's why I say *'Live the dream,'* don't tell me you don't have the time, we all have the same twenty four hours. Although Bauby's book is a memoir of his life, it reminds me how little time we have, and how precious our lives are. Each one counts and to live our dreams, and hold life itself dear to our hearts. Jean-Dominique Bauby died of a heart attack on March 9th 1997 two days after the book was published in France.

I can only say go out and read this book, and learn how a man coped within a shell, living the suffocation of a diving bell existence and at the same time releasing the butterflies of his imagination to the world.

So I say *'live the dream,'* and go out and do whatever it is you want from life. Let you mind be free to dream, and in those dreams that may come, do not say I have no time, for we all have the same time the same twenty four hours. So remember what Confucius said, *"It's a fool that never reads a book."* As I turn another corner in my life.

It's Never Too Late

Just a Few Pennies More

"A penny saved is a penny earned,"
by Benjamin Franklin

Have you ever had the experience of losing everything and having to start again penniless? Pull up a chair folks, you coffee junkies, milkshake hussies and the teletubbies. Suck on that straw and a banana milkshake for me, because I have a story to tell. It was the summer of 2010, and I woke up in a financial nightmare. But, it was my fault, having bipolar and unable sometimes to control my actions it was sometimes easy come and easy go, bit like a banker.

Being penniless with all the problems, and the debt with no money, it's no fun, right? Not even enough to buy a cup of coffee. Zilch, that's all I had just a few pennies in my pocket some days. And, I was no magician able to pull a bunny out of my hat.

What would you do when you have bills to pay and nothing in the bank? In fact, you're in overdraft territory? Well, to make you think for a moment – take a deep breath and relax. There are plenty of examples I could list, from totally insane to the bizarre.

The Prodigy song Poison on their album *Music for the Jilted Generation* and the lyrics "*I got the poison, I got the remedy*," reminds me of a totally insane way of dealing with this scenario. But, hey, a great track. Don't get me wrong suicide is never the answer; I'm just listing the options not advocating them.

Jeffrey Archer the author wrote a book called, *Not a penny more, Not a penny less*, it was his first novel, and he dug himself out of a big financial hole after losing a fortune as a casualty in a fraudulent investment scheme. The book was a success and he has written best sellers since.

Being down on your luck it just goes to show what can happen if you have the balls and energy to get back up there again? You might retort, not everyone can write a book. Well, you could be right; it's a yes and no answer. Yes, you can write a book, and, no, it may not be a bestseller. Oh, I forgot to mention it will take effort and few sleepless nights, so if you like your beauty sleep then it's probably not a good idea.

And, if you have any doubts about what you can do because there're always a few sceptics around those doubting Thomas's who refuse to believe what's possible here's the answer. Today, while shopping in the local mall a picked up a book its title was "*How to talk to girls.*" You can always do with some extra tips, I was thinking.

My biggest problem has not been how to talk to girls, but how to pick the right ones. Seriously, some of my girlfriend's have been more manic then me. Recently, I had one girlfriend, who wanted to marry me after knowing me for only a week that's either commitment or totally bonkers?

Curious cat, I turned the book over to find out the cost. It turns out that the book was written by an eight year old boy, his name is Alec Greven. So if you still have any doubts about what you can do just carry on sucking on that straw you never know it may just send you to sleep, and then who knows what dreams may come.

Anyway, lets continue with the story, it's a story I would rather forget but it needs to be told. Only a few months ago now, shortly before writing this book I walked into a charity shop to buy a book. With just a few pennies in my pocket, not even enough to buy a cup of coffee, though I did haggle with the sales assistant to buy a book with what I had.

I looked at the sales assistant in the charity shop straight in the eyes, and said, *'I haven't got what you're asking.'*

'Well, it is a charity shop,' he said
'Why do you think I'm here,' I said with a smile.

Grudgingly he replied, *'Go on then just for you.'* I was pleased at least I had a book for the weekend to keep me occupied. I was flat broke, but it felt like it would be a good weekend somehow reading my book. Now, I did have the prospect of what was lurking down the couch to replenish my funds.

Desperate times you could say. Well, yes, I was broke, and living at the door of the hungry man's. Let me explain, the hungry man's is what my father would say if you needed government handouts. And, I definitely needed some handouts some of that tax money I had paid all the years before.

Sure my government handouts were due to come through the next day for the month, but even then I was living in overdraft territory. Every month for just a few days I was in credit by a small amount if I was lucky, even catching a bus to the city to watch people spending their money was a luxury I couldn't afford.

Reading second-hand books, watching TV and occasionally finding something to sell on EBay were the highlights to the passing days and weeks for me. Part of the problem for me with bipolar is not being able to control unremitting spending sprees until it was too late. You become a spending junkie, and the only rehab available is going broke. My condition made managing money extremely difficult, which is often a common characteristic of the disorder. I was worst than a banker on speed. The only difference from me and a banker, I was spending my money. At least, they get to spend other people's money, which is a lot healthier.

Then one day I started to list the things in my mind which I had bought, takeaway meals here, video rentals there, the odd T-shirt and many other items I could have done without over the previous months. The money I had given away to friends and family over the years. It was crazy; I had wasted so much money just here and there. Then I started to think deeper, and then I remembered. Oh, shit, I remembered the beauty treatment fiasco.

Of course, there was this time when I spent the cost a holiday on beauty products I didn't need. You can laugh, what did I need beauty products for? I'm over fifty and lucky I still have some hair on my head. Walking through the local shopping mall back to the multi-storey car park, back a year and a half ago one day I was stopped by an attractive girl on a concessions counter selling an expensive range of beauty products. I know what you're thinking, and you are partially right. I'm a sucker! But I do have bipolar, which means controlling spending is very difficult sometimes.

Sure enough, I was sold, lock stock and too bloody late. Well, you can laugh, and you should because I ended up buying probably enough beauty products to last a girl several years and them some, and I didn't even need them. I am not going to get any better looking even if had a thousand face packs.

Eventually, I gave the lot to my daughter, not that she really needed them either but she laughed also. Buying this stuff was crazy; there was more chance of me having a facelift in Thailand, than applying a cleansing face pack and looking like a Zulu warrior with face paint ready for war.

Thinking: *I knew this episode would come to bite me in the ass when I didn't have any money.* Clearly, at the time something had been wrong with me, I couldn't stop myself buying all that yuck. I even had to ask the sales girl the way to the car park, yet I knew this shopping mall like the back of my hand, which should have been a big indicator that something was wrong.

Anyway, it was my fault because I hadn't been careful with money when I had some, and, now, I hoped I had learnt my lesson. Letting my bank account get overdrawn when I didn't even have any savings to raid was madness.

My money was gone – all gone, just a few pennies in my pocket, all spent above all on things I didn't need. For my part what an idiot I had been. The malaise in my fortunes lasted several months, and it taught me a lesson of how to manage my money more carefully in the future, if I was going to avoid the proverbial work house.

You quickly learn that it's not a pleasant experience when you don't have any money in your pocket. Well, relax your mind and take a deep breath for a moment.

Hopefully you'll never have to endure this predicament but you never know when the inheritance runs out or that top job just disappears into a cloud of ether. Don't count on anything or else you may wake up with even less than you thought you had the day before, and that was bad enough. And don't second guess Sod's Law, Murphy's Law or the mother-in-law because they can always play the part when least expected.

Its difficult to teach people new tricks – I know because I have tried many times and I lack the patience of a Saint, so all I can say is everything comes at a price and most things worthwhile take effort and time. At times I felt like a child that needed to grow up.

Adapting to new ideas is easy for children as they don't have a lifetime of assumptions to deal with. So don't make the assumption like I did thinking I would be okay financially. As adults we make assumptions all the time which are invariable wrong, which inhibit our ability to learn and accept new ideas. Well, this was one lesson I hoped I had learnt.

There is no easy answers just remember to look after your money, and don't waste it along the way. I found that it was a lot harder to save money than to spend it. A penny saved is a penny earned and not having money made me appreciate money in a different way – how not to waste it when you have money that was the first lesson, and a hard lesson to learn. Now, whenever I see an attractive lady on a concessions counter trying to sell me beauty products I just keep on walking.

I Took the Plunge

"Action is the antidote to despair,"
by Joan Baez

It was the middle of 2010 and I had wasted the previous 6 months doing absolutely nothing. The manic depression had remerged and taken over my life again. But I was determined somehow I was going to try and conquer its power over me always knowing it wouldn't be a final solution. I wasn't looking for the silver bullet just another strategy, which I could use to fight the foe, that black cloud.

At times, I was very isolated alone in my apartment. One day would run into another and the weeks would pass. The black cloud had come again to try and take me under. It's difficult to explain how sometimes everything would seem hopeless and everything a tried didn't work. It was a spiral and I was going down.

Even though I would go for walks along the cliffs, and sit and watch the ocean I didn't have any contact with anyone. I wasn't socialising, something that had crept up upon me like a spider. The more I thought about it the more I felt marginalised.

The black cloud had taken over my life. I was more alone than anytime in my life. At least, before I would go dancing once or twice a week, but, now, I wasn't doing anything to get out of this modernity.

I decided I needed to join a group. My mental health counsellor originally broached the idea at one of the regular sessions with him over the previous two and half years. Recently, the only contact with anyone except for usual shopping trips to buy groceries was my counsellor. Sometimes in the space of two to three weeks the only real conversation I would have with anyone was my counsellor. I needed to get out there and meet the world again head on.

The hermit existence I had been living was not me, but for some reason I had become a social leper again. That's the problem with bipolar one minute you are right at the front of the class ready to put your hand up the next you're at the back hiding. It's difficult to find the middle ground and stay there. The first thing I did was to stop smoking the wacky backy partly because I could not afford it but more importantly I made up my mind I didn't need it.

The wacky backy was holding me back and I knew it, forcing me to stay indoors because I would feel paranoid if I went outside and people saw me. Besides, I had only recently started smoking wacky backy again after many years without the weed. I wanted to get out there again and not have any handicaps. I was determined I would follow a prescribed medication routine and not a self-medication one, which had not always been the case.

To find out if there were any local support groups for bipolar sufferers I decided to do some research on the Internet, and sure enough there was. I was able to track down the details of the local bipolar support group in my area, something I should have done a lot sooner. When I phoned to find out the day and time of the next meeting the nice lady on phone explained, I would be very welcome, which was just what I needed.

So that was the start, I could not wait, in my head I knew this would be new beginning somehow. I can remember saving money for the bus fare because at the time I was living on a shoe string, and I wanted to go and make that first step.

Joining the support group I got to hear about other workshops, which again was another excuse for me to get out of the house. I think joining a bipolar support group is a good idea, and one way of helping to relive the stress of dealing with the condition. I only wish

I had joined a support group earlier instead of waiting several years before I took the plunge.

Listening to other people explain their stories helped me understand myself better. It was also useful excuse for me to get out of the house and meet new people and maybe make new friends. One thing I didn't do was pretend that I was the only person that mattered in these group sessions.

Obviously, each support group will have their own structure but they are usually informal and don't put on any pressure for you to attend – its up to you whether you turn up. I found the local support group was useful for me as it was a stepping stone for other events that I became aware of.

These other events and workshops allowed me to mix and to socialise with other people with similar problems. Gradually, I started to come out of my shell, and I could feel the benefits as the black cloud began to disappear.

I would recommend self help groups to those who feel they are ready to let the outside world into their lives. I was well aware about setting my own boundaries about what I would divulge to the group at anytime –this gave me control and something that is important to maintain. I welcomed the opportunity just to listen to other people talk about how they felt.

Until you begin to trust your fellow group members I felt what I said would be minimal. I sat there most of time and just listened to others until I felt confident with them. It was good to feel part of the world again. I could identify and sympathise with other bipolar sufferers. I began to trust them and so let them trust me. As everything that is said in these group sessions is confidential, it's important that they also trust you.

Joining a support group certainly helped me, and though it's no silver bullet I can confidently recommend this as another strategy in combating that black cloud that bipolar sufferers have to live with.

It's Never Too Late

Getting Old Sucks!

"The surest sign of age is loneliness,"
by Amos Bronson Alcott

I can remember the first time a heard the phrase, *'getting old sucks!'* My mum still uses the phrase, and in lots of ways she's right. You have a lot more aches and pains and you can't always do what you did when you were younger. Plus, there's the dreaded curse of loneliness which can affect us all at some point in our lives, especially as we get older.

I can remember as a child I would think that people I saw that were over forty were old, and now I'm over fifty I don't try to think about it. No! Seriously, there are a few more aches and pains, I think I had those when I was young, getting old is part of life's mystery, accept it and try to enjoy it.

Life's a journey, and when I think about it you are here to learn and love. I'm glad I got this far, and hope that whatever happens it will be the love I left behind that really mattered.

Most people want answers to why and what is their purpose, and I think I've already answered that one; it's the love you give and leave behind that's the most important gift you have. There is a constant change in all of our lives, as we grow old we can find this difficult to deal with.

Sometimes it's our appearance that makes us unhappy. Yet, we are all born with different personalities, skills and gifts that we can appreciate when we learn how to find them. We all want more. Yet, if we learn to want less, we can also find an inner calm and peace.

The Buddha found the supreme liberation in what he called *Nirvana,* replacing suffering with a peace of mind that he believed everyone was able to achieve.

It's up to you whether to follow a Buddhist approach to life or any other religion or doctrine, and that is your choice. I can only say what works for me, and that's the philosophy I've lived with to cope with the black clouds of my depression.

I do believe that it's up to the individual what they want to believe in, and what religion they want to follow if any. Freedom of expression I believe is important right; for our minds to be able to explore, to think outside the boundaries of any particular doctrine.

I am a street corner philosopher, and the way I see it my Jekyll and Hyde personality is always pulling me in one direction or another. I have had to cope with manic phases – a learnt the hard way, I don't know all the answers, and I don't pretend to know.

A balanced body and mind is my philosophy. At times I have led the rock style life, but without the mansion to sleep off the all night benders of booze and girls, the self-medication, hell I am no angel some of the things I have got up to I don't think I will be telling my grand children anytime soon!

Just recently I phoned my Aunty Kitty in Blackpool, I hadn't spoken to her for several years. She was to glad to hear from me, and understood everything I said even though she was the grand age of 96. We spoke for a considerable length of time and she remembered the last time I saw her when I took her and my mum out to dinner with my girlfriend Gill when I was living up north in Sunderland.

We laughed about different things I said, and she told me that she had no regrets about her life even though she had been married three times! She made me laugh, and asked me why I hadn't remarried; I told her that I was still looking for the right one. I could hear in her voice and what she said, even though she told me about her failing eyesight and all the other aches and pains of old age, that she had enjoyed reaching old age with no regrets.

Aunty Kitty had the right attitude that reaching old age should be a chalice of no regrets. If we are given this gift of old age then we should respect it for what it is. Reaching old age has given us a chance for us to enjoy who we are, and to live life to the full and give back to those less fortunate.

Sure, we all want to be young again, but I feel like I'm twenty inside that's how my mind feels that is the important thing. By thinking younger we can stay younger in our hearts. Of course, we can spend lots of money on plastic surgery and other beauty treatments that is your choice, but look around you, we can't stop getting old we should accept and enjoy it.

Sometimes, you can live in a place for many years and never notice the noise of the passing traffic, until eventually one day you realize you have to move on. In reaching old age we find a chalice of wisdom which you can now use to benefit everyone. I know when you get older you tend to moan a lot more, but I think that is just a myth.

When I was younger I may have needed to keep up with the Jones's, now I don't see the need. William Shakespeare talked about the seven stages of man. Well, I am at that stage when I don't care if the brand I'm wearing is by Romeo or Juliet as long as it looks good, fits well, and I don't have to kill for it.

I have stopped buying brand items and celebrity labels because I don't feel the need to impress anyone, and I can't afford them. Sure, an expensive pen looks good in a cabinet or on the desk, and even in the hand; but the words you write don't mean more. Who would know if I wrote a letter with a Mont Blanc or a cheap alternative?

For me, owning something is not about the status but its necessity. Hey, if someone wants to send me a Mont Blanc feel free – I will try it out. I don't think it will improve my hand writing that's still the same chaotic scribble, I prefer it that way – its me, its who I am.

As a kid its awful when you find out you die, it's okay because in living you get a chance to learn and to love, and to be loved and it's that love that is remembered. You don't live forever, but as the Buddha said, while you're here you can seek that *Nirvana* which ever way you get there.

Being born, growing old, getting sick and dieing are part of living, being old is a chalice that holds so much more that is up to us how we choose to live our lives.

End of the Book

"Truly great madness can not be achieved without significant intelligence,"
by Henrik Tikkanen

I wrote this book to tell my story and how manic depression has affected my life. I hope that my philosophy and strategies that I use everyday can help other people who suffer with the same condition come to terms with the rollercoaster ride.

I have been on a journey dealing with the affects of a disorder which can destroy as well as create opportunities previously unnoticed. I hope I have been able to demonstrate this philosophy as a way of learning to look at life with open eyes and being able to grasp new opportunities. The search for truth and knowledge can awaken a new zest for life in you, and I hope this truly finds you, as it did me.

I am often reminded by what Confucius said about how to live your life so that you can be a better person. Confucius said, *"Always speak with true words, and if asked for little and you have the power to give then you should, with these three things you will go close to the Gods."*

I have tried to follow these wise words with positive action whenever I am presented with this challenge. I do believe these steps are important in becoming a better person so that you can help others. I know you can't help everyone but it's good to help where you can, and to know that you're making positive improvements to someone's life.

When I was first diagnosed with bipolar, at first, I would not accept the diagnosis. It wasn't until I did my own research into the condition that I began to come to terms with the disorder. In some ways, it helped me come to terms with my situation as I learnt more about the subject. I learnt that there are many people from all walks of life dealing everyday with the disorder.

They reckon there is about one percent of the population who might have some kind of bipolar. As I started to read more and more about bipolar I wasn't satisfied until I understood its implications, and finding ways of coping with the problem.

It became a comfort to me to read the stories on the internet of people coping with bipolar. I found that there were many similarities in the stories posted – such as how it was common to have a lack of control about spending money, and how you could be on cloud nine one minute and in the depths of depression the next – even with the appropriate medication taken.

I even looked into the medical research currently being carried out. It seems there are two schools of thought. Essentially, there's no substantial statistical evidence to back up either assertion. One half of the medical establishment believes that bipolar is basically a biological problem – maybe a defective gene, the other believes it could be physiological just a product of your environment. It's hard to say one way or the other – I believe it could be a product of both – an inherited gene - a chemical imbalance and how your environment has affected your life.

Although, not enough research has been carried out to determine how the disorder manifests itself. Mental illness is still a major issue for many of us and needs to be addressed for future generations.

I read many interesting stories how individuals had arrived through their illness at a point where in some cases their own family and friends miss-understood the condition and offered no support. Family and friends of sufferers often knew very little about the disorder and so found it difficult to deal with. There was a feeling of abandonment in some of the stories. The lack of knowledge by family or friends can easily leave many sufferers feeling lost or inadequate.

One benefit of the Internet has been the wealth of information available and how easily it was for me to access when I needed to understand for myself what the hell was going on with me.

The first-hand accounts of individuals who told their stories allowed me to link the behaviours and similarities. By doing this I was able to understand what to possibly expect, and it certainly helped me in my darkest moments to come to terms with bipolar. The crazy stories that were told even though they were sad I could identify with, allowing me to break through what was like a black cloud hanging over me at the time.

Look at new beginnings as an opportunity to explore one self, and don't look at any setbacks as a disaster, but as an opportunity to open new doors. Who knows what will lead from opening up new doors previously closed. Confucius said, "*The first step is always the hardest.*"

I close this book with a message that I hope will stay with you – *the truth never lies.* As you search for the truth a deeper knowledge will grow, and give you a better understanding of your future. With this new knowledge you will begin to hold your own destiny and not be under the control of others.

It's been a struggle these past few years to know how to write this book – but in the end I think I've achieved what I set out to do.

The End

It's Never Too Late

Simply

"Open the door and look out.
Come with me to the end.
Search the skies, and open your eyes.
Follow me to the end. "

Poem written by Anthony Fox © 1999

It's Never Too Late

CPSIA information can be obtained at www.ICGtesting.com
Printed in the USA
BVOW07s2224131113

336211BV00001B/30/P

9 781783 820092